WORLD WAR II FROM ORIG

BY AIR TO BATTLE

The Official History of the British Paratroops in World War II

EDITED AND INTRODUCED BY BOB CARRUTHERS

Pen & Sword
AVIATION

This edition published in 2012 by
Pen & Sword Aviation
An imprint of
Pen & Sword Books Ltd
47 Church Street
Barnsley
South Yorkshire
S70 2AS

First published in Great Britain in 2012 in digital format by
Coda Books Ltd.

Copyright © Coda Books Ltd, 2012
Published under licence by Pen & Sword Books Ltd.

ISBN 978 1 78159 113 0

Originally published in 1945 as "By Air to Battle - The Official Account of the
British First and Sixth Airborne Divisions" in London by His Majesty's Stationery
Office.

Printed and bound by CPI Group (UK) Ltd, Croydon, CR0 4YY

Pen & Sword Books Ltd incorporates the Imprints of Pen & Sword Aviation, Pen &
Sword Family History, Pen & Sword Maritime, Pen & Sword Military, Pen &
Sword Discovery, Pen & Sword Politics, Pen & Sword Atlas, Pen & Sword
Archaeology, Wharncliffe Local History, Wharncliffe True Crime, Wharncliffe
Transport, Pen & Sword Select, Pen & Sword Military Classics, Leo Cooper, The
Praetorian Press, Claymore Press, Remember When, Seaforth Publishing and
Frontline Publishing

For a complete list of Pen & Sword titles please contact
PEN & SWORD BOOKS LIMITED
47 Church Street, Barnsley, South Yorkshire, S70 2AS, England
E-mail: enquiries@pen-and-sword.co.uk
Website: www.pen-and-sword.co.uk

CONTENTS

INTRODUCTION

FIRST PUBLISHED IN 1945 and comprising a compilation of fascinating primary accounts of airborne combat as told by the very men who fought in the action, 'By Air to Battle' is the official history of Airborne operations by British Paratroops in World War II. Spanning the introduction of the Central Landing Establishment to the end of the war, we follow the heroic exploits of the British First and Sixth Airborne Divisions.

'By Air to Battle' is an inspiring and at times very comic description of the true events that took place at such historic conflicts as Arnhem, the Rhine, Normandy and Bruneval as well as the Airborne forces in North Africa, Sicily and Italy. This is a must-read for any military history enthusiast.

Bob Carruthers

CHAPTER 1

"THE WONDERFUL AIR OF DAWN"

A FEW MINUTES AFTER one o'clock in the morning of June 6th, 1944, Monsieur Georges Gondrée, a Norman innkeeper, was awakened by his wife. " At that time we slept," he explained, "in separate rooms ; not because we wanted to, but because that was the best way of preventing German troops from being billeted upon us. She said to me, ' Get up. Don 't you hear what's happening ? Open the window.' I was sleepy and it took me some little time to grasp what she meant. She repeated, ' Get up. Listen. It sounds like wood breaking' I opened the window and looked out."

The window which Gondrée opened was on the first floor of a café on the outskirts of Benouville, a village in Normandy. It is situated a few yards from the western end of the steel swing bridge which there crosses the Canal de Caen and which by decree of the French Government will always be known as 'Pegasus Bridge.' "It was moonlight," he continued, "but I could see nothing, though I did hear snapping and crunching sounds."

A German Sentry was standing at the bridgehead a few yards away, and Gondrée, whose wife is an Alsatian and speaks excellent German, suggested that she should ask him what was happening. She leant out of the window and did so, while her husband observed his face, clearly visible in the moonlight. His features were working, his eyes wide with fear. For a moment he did not speak, and " then saw that he was literally struck dumb by terror. At last he stammered out the one word 'Parachutists.' "

"What a pity," said the wife to her husband, "those English

lads (gars) will be captured," for they both thought at that moment that what the sentry had seen was the crew of a bomber baling out. Almost immediately firing broke out and tracers began to flash across the night sky. Having two small children, the Gondrées took refuge in the cellar, where they remained for some time listening to the spasmodic sounds of battle outside. Presently there was a knock on the front door and a voice in German called on them to leave the café and walk in front of German troops. This German version of "Dilly dally, come and be killed" did not appeal to them and they remained where they were until Madame Gondrée, clad only in her nightdress, and shivering with cold, urged her husband to go up and see what was happening. Gondree did so. "I am not a brave man," he said, "and I did not want to be shot, so I went upstairs on all fours and crawled to the first-floor window. There I heard talk outside but could not distinguish the words, so I pushed open the window and peeped out cautiously. ... I saw in front of the café two soldiers sitting near my petrol pump with a corpse between them."

Men with coal-black faces

Somewhat unnerved by this sight, Gondrée could not clearly understand the reply of the soldiers to his hail in French, but he thought one of them said : "Armée de l'air," and the other "English flieger." "I still thought," his account goes on, "that they belonged to the crew of a crashed bomber, but I was worried by the clothes they had on and also by the fact that they seemed to be wearing black masks." This was scarcely reassuring, but the innkeeper, mindful of the danger in which he and his family appeared to stand, determined to continue his investigations. He went to another window, this one giving on to the canal bank which runs at right angles to the road crossing the bridge. Peering out, he saw two more soldiers who "lifted their weapons and pointed them at me. By then there were a number of flares burning in the sky, so that I could see quite plainly. One of the soldiers said to me, 'Vous civile?' I replied 'Oui, Oui,' and added something else which I don't remember. The soldier answered, 'Vous civile?' and after a moment I realised that these were the only words of French he knew. I was for twelve years a bank clerk in Lloyds Bank in Paris and I therefore speak good English, but I did not wish to let that fact be known at that moment, for I was not sure who they were. One of them then put his finger to his lips and gestured with his hands to indicate that I should close the shutter. This I did and went back to the cellar. "

Nothing more happened for some time till the Gondrées heard sounds of digging in their vegetable garden outside. They looked through a hole in the cellar and "there was the wonderful air of dawn coming up over the land." Vague figures were moving about. They seemed peaceful enough, and to Gondrée's astonishment " I could hear no guttural orders, which I always associated with a German working-party. I turned to my wife and said : 'Ils ne gueulent pas comme d'habitude.' The light grew stronger and I began to have serious doubts whether the people I could see were in fact the crew of a bomber ; their behaviour seemed to me to be very strange. I told my wife to go to the hole in the cellar, listen and tell me if they were speaking German. She did so and presently said that she could not understand what they were saying. Then I in my turn listened, and my heart began to beat quicker for I thought I heard the words 'all right.' "

Presently there were further sounds of knocking, and this time Gondrée opened the door, to be confronted by two men with coal-black faces. He then realised that it was paint, not masks, which they were wearing. They inquired in French whether there were any Germans in the house. He answered "no" and brought them in to the bar and thence, with some reluctance on their part, which he overcame by smiles and gestures, to the cellar. Arrived there, he pointed to his wife and two children " for a moment there was silence ; then one soldier turned to the other and said 'It's all right, chum.' At last I knew they were English and burst into tears."

Madame Gondrée and her children at once kissed the soldiers and as a result were immediately covered with black camouflage paint.

Monsieur and Madame Gondrée were, in all probability, the first French civilians to see British airborne troops, harbingers of freedom and victory, when they landed by parachute and from gliders on the morning of the Allied invasion of Europe. It is the story of two divisions of those troops, how they came in to being, how they were trained, and of what befell them from the first uncertain beginnings in 1940, through the tragedy and triumph of Arnhem, to the refulgent victory of the Rhine that is here set down.

CHAPTER 2

GETTING INTO HARNESS: THE PARACHUTIST'S TRAINING

O N JUNE 22nd, 1940, the Prime Minister sent a brief instruction to his Chief of Staff. " We ought," ' he wrote, " to have a corps of at least five thousand parachute troops .... I hear something is being done already to form such a corps but only, I believe, on a very small scale. Advantage must be taken of the summer to train these forces, who can none the less play their part meanwhile as shock troops in home defence. Pray let me have a note from the War Office on the subject."

Immediate action was taken, for two days later Major J. F. Rock, Royal Engineers, was summoned to the War Office and ordered to take charge of the military organisation of British airborne forces. How he was to do so, of what those forces were to consist, what arms they were to carry, what method was to be used to train them and to transport them to war, were not explained. " It was impossible," records Rock in his diary, " to get any information as to policy or task." Rock was a regular soldier, but his acquaintance with aircraft was not more intimate than that of a frequent passenger. He knew nothing of parachutes or gliders beyond what he had read or was soon to read concerning their use by the enemy in the attacks delivered against Holland and Belgium six weeks before.

Goering had began the organisation of airborne forces as far back as 1936, and the Germans placed great reliance on them to create confusion in the ranks of the enemy at the crucial moment and the crucial point. The possibilities of this new form of warfare were obviously very great, and it was therefore high time to plan ahead, so that when the moment came and the tables were turned, the British Army should have at its disposal a force capable of achieving all that the enemy had achieved and much more.

It was not the Germans but our Russian allies who first realized how airborne forces might be of use. Like the yeomen of England in the 14th century, who made shooting with the long-bow a national pastime leading to national victories on the field of battle, the Russians made popular the sport of parachute jumping. Towers were set up all over the territory of Russia, and by leaping from their summits old and young sought to acquire proficiency in parachuting. There is a story, which is surely ben trovato, that a grandmother of eighty jumped followed by her grandson of six ; the first made a perfect landing ; the second was badly hurt.

By 1936 the Russian Army possessed a trained force of parachute troops which in the summer manoeuvres of that year dropped 1,200 men led by a General, 150 machine-guns, and eighteen light field guns before, among others, the eyes of General Wavell. On returning to England he reported that, "if I had not witnessed the descents I could not have believed such an operation possible."

The Central Landing Establishment is formed

All this and more was in the mind of Major Rock as he travelled to a certain Royal Air Force station, to take up his new, ill-defined, but extremely important duties. On arrival he found a useful satellite airfield close by, where in peacetime a private landing ground had been laid out for the use of the aircraft in the possession of its owner. It was at these two places that the Central Landing School, to be known from September 1940 as the Central Landing Establishment, began to play its peculiar and vital part in transforming the country's strong powers of defence into still stronger powers of attack.

The change in name was perhaps an attempt to cure the confusion which at first existed alike in the official and the public mind concerning the new organisation's correct postal address. Shortly after his arrival Rock, by then a Lieutenant-Colonel, received a letter from the War Office addressed " Central Laundry," while Private Crane, an early recruit, was thought by one of his correspondents to be attending the " Central Sunday School. "

Rock was soon at work with a number of Air Force colleagues, of whom Wing Commanders L. A. Strange, D.S.O., M.C., D.E.C., and Sir Nigel Norman, Bt., C.B.E., were the chief. To these three, two of whom, Norman and Rock, were to die for her, England owes a great debt. Together with others of a like mind they strove with every kind of difficulty, ranging from lack of equipment to lack of understanding ; and in the end they prevailed.

Since it was to be operated by the R.A.F., Group Captain L. G. Harvey commanded the Establishment, which soon included a Development Unit, a Glider Training Squadron and a Parachute School under Group Captain Newnham. The first experiments in parachute jumping began on July 13th, 1940. Among the instructors, most of them enthusiastic amateurs, was Warrant Officer, then Flight Sergeant, Brereton, who had been a fabric worker of the R.A.F. in peacetime, and whose skill and great physical strength were to stand more than one pupil in good stead. Major J. Lander, who until his death in action in 1943 was responsible for a number of successful devices, mostly connected with the dropping of weapons and ammunition, was also soon on the scene. In those early days the instructors belonged partly to the Army, partly to the Royal Air Force but as time went on and the Establishment developed they came to be drawn entirely from the Physical Training Branch of the R.A.F. In their ranks there have been and still are, men belonging to many and varied professions. A number are schoolmasters, professional footballers and boxers, and with them among others are a road cycle champion, a circus acrobat, a "Wall of Death" rider and a male dancer from the Ballet. These men, between them, had jumped more than 16,000 times by the end of 1944, and all of them have been on operations against the enemy.

At first, the Central Landing Establishment was conspicuous mainly for an almost total lack of the equipment necessary to train parachute soldiers, glider pilots, and air-landing troops. Information was equally scanty. A damaged parachute and jumping helmet captured from the Germans were the only models available, and for aircraft there were four Whitley Mark IIs, which were seldom simultaneously serviceable. Material in the form of parachutes was presently provided by the energetic labours of two commercial firms, trade rivals, but firmly united in their determination to endow their country with the finest airborne equipment which could be devised.

The principle of the statichute - that is, a parachute which opens automatically was already known, and was rapidly being developed till it became as near fool-proof as any man-made device can be.

That accidents were not altogether avoidable is shown by the official report of Captain P. E. Bromley-Martin on what happened to him on February 4th, 1941. During a dropping exercise he jumped fourth, after his colleague, Major H. O. Wright. " The next recollection I have," he states, " is that of Major Wright with parachute open and canopy fully filled, some 150 feet directly above me. My parachute had at that time not fully opened and I had then the gravest doubts as to whether it would fully function before it had been repacked. I was unable to devise a method of repacking it within the limited time at my disposal. As I was also unable to think of any satisfactory means of assisting the contraption to perform the functions which I had been led to expect were automatic, in my submission I had no alternative but to fall earthwards at, I believe, the rate of thirty-two feet per second accelerating to the maximum speed of 176 feet .... This I did .... Having dropped a certain distance, my parachute suddenly opened and I made a very light landing. ' '

While parachutes and their accompanying apparatus were being manufactured, the earliest recruits' - they came mostly from the newly raised No. 2 Commando and were all volunteers-were introduced to the art of jumping by being made to stand on a platform situated at the rear of the Whitley, the turret having first been removed. Crouching there, the jumper released his parachute and was then dragged off the platform into space by the slipstream of the aircraft. Before the recruits performed this feat their instructors had first to learn to do so.

"For four days," says Captain M. A. Lindsay, "there had been a strong wind. For four days I had felt as if my skin had been cleaned every morning with ether; in preparation for the surgeon's knife. The fifth day was calm .... We climbed into the aircraft and sat on the floor of the fuselage. The engines roared and we took off. I noticed how moist the palms of my hands were. I wished I didn't always feel slightly sick in an aircraft. I remembered a man I met years ago in some bar ; he told me he had once been paid a pound a piece by the Chilean Government for testing thirty parachutes. Not enough, I thought to myself at that moment, not nearly enough.

"It seemed an age, but it cannot have been more than ten minutes when the instructor beckoned to me. The Germans have a chucker-out in their aircraft for the encouragement of nervous recruits. Flight Sergeant Brereton, six foot two inches, would have made a good Abetzer. I began to make my way down the fuselage towards him, screwing myself up to do so. I crawled on my hands and knees into the rear-gunner's turret, the back of which had been removed. I tried not to overbalance and fall out, nor to look at the landscape speeding across below me as I turned to face forward again.

"I now found myself on a small platform about a foot square, at the very back of the plane, hanging on like grim death to the bar under which I had had such difficulty in crawling. The two rudders were a few feet away on either side of me ; behind me was nothing whatsoever. As soon as I raised myself to full height, I found that I was to all purposes outside the plane, the slipstream of air in my face almost blowing me out. I quickly huddled up, my head bent down and pressed into the capacious bosom of the Flight Sergeant. He held up his hand for me to watch. I was about to make a " pull-off," opening my parachute which would not pull me off until fully developed- a procedure which was calculated to fill me with such confidence that I should be only too ready to leap smartly out of the aircraft on all subsequent occasions.

"The little light at the side changed from yellow to red. I was undeniably frightened, though at the same time filled with a fearful joy. The light changed to green and down fell his hand. I put my right hand across to the D ring in front of my left side and pulled sharply. A pause of nearly a second and then a jerk on each shoulder. I was whisked off backwards and swung through nearly 180 degrees, beneath the canopy and up the other side.

But I was quite oblivious to this. I had something akin to a black-out. At any rate, the first thing I was conscious of after the jerk on my shoulders was to find myself, perhaps four seconds later, sitting up in my harness and floating down to earth. The only sensation I registered was one of utter astonishment at finding myself so suddenly in this remarkable and ridiculous position.

"I looked up and saw the silken canopy billowing in the air currents - a thing of beauty as the sun shone on and through it. I reached down and eased the harness straps from the more vulnerable parts of my body. I looked down, reflecting that this was certainly the second greatest thrill in a man's life. Suddenly

I realized that the ground was coming up very rapidly. Before I knew what had happened I was sprawling on the ground, having taken a bump but no hurt. As I got to my feet, a feeling of exhilaration began to till me."

Two other pupils of Brereton, jumping about the same time, were not so fortunate. Regimental Sergeant-Major Manzie hit the ground with his head and was carried off unconscious. The next to jump was Captain J. Dawes, O.B.E. "'Take your time,' said Flight Sergeant Brereton," he records, "'we'll make a dummy run first .... We are almost over the airfield now.' With a great effort of will I dared to look down .... To my horror I saw five hundred feet below a tiny stretcher with a dark, motionless figure ..., Brereton must have seen it too for he looked hard at me and said, 'There's nothing to worry about. If you like I'll pull the rip-cord for you myself." 'I'm all right . . just tell me what to do.' 'Watch my hand then, and, when you see it fall, pull the handle upward and outward.'

'O.K.,' I said, 'you mean like this?' 'Not now, you bloody fool' - but it was too late. I'd gone. Three hours later the search party found me, six miles away from the dropping zone, hanging helplessly from the highest branches of a clump of trees."

The parachute soldier's equipment

This method of parachuting of was not always safe, and accidents happened, the first to be fatal occurring as early as July 25th, 1940.

On one occasion the parachute of a pupil, instead of streaming out and being filled with the slipstream, blew back and smothered him with its silken folds while he was still clinging to the platform. To keep him there, Flight Sergeant Brereton sat firmly upon his head and chest until the Whitley made a landing and deposited them, shaken and bruised, but safe on the airfield.

On another occasion, during an exercise in Scotland, a parachute soldier made his jump from a Whitley through an aperture, but the pack on his back did not open and he remained on the end of the strop, being towed through the air behind the aircraft. This mishap was not noticed by its crew, who could only see that all the strops had duly passed through the hole, and were not aware that one of them was still loaded. The Whitley made a normal landing and by singular good fortune the parachutist on tow struck the ground in such a way as to cause the shock to be taken by his parachute pack. He was dragged some yards ; then at last the strop released. He rolled over two or three times and got to his feet, unhurt.

Gradually the modern type of harness was evolved and the modern method of jumping. This is through a hole in the floor of the aircraft or if it should be a Dakota (C.47) it is through the door. The' method may thus be described. With his feet on the edge, the parachutist sits, crouches or stands ready to jump. His clothes, though seemingly complicated, are simple to wear and designed to give him the maximum warmth in the air and the maximum mobility on the ground. He wears a parachute harness over his jumping jacket. Beneath that is the equipment which he will carry into battle. This in turn is worn over his parachute smock, a garment made of windproof material with large pockets. Beneath the smock is an ordinary battle dress, but the trousers have very wide exterior pockets. At first his boots were provided with thick crepe rubber soles, but lately this has been found unnecessary, and now ordinary army boots were worn. The all-important parachute knife, with which the parachute soldier can cut himself free if necessary, is strapped to the right leg. On his head is a special form of helmet shaped like a flat, circular cheese. This is used for practice jumps. On operations a steel helmet not unlike a bowler hat, but without a brim, is worn.

To the parachute harness is attached a bag carried on the back. In it is housed the parachute in an internal bag divided into two compartments. The outside bag remains attached to the harness ; the inside is pulled violently from it by a static line, which is a length of webbing, of which one end is attached strongly to the inner bag. At the other end is a metal D ring which engages a hook attached to the end of the strop. The strop is also made of webbing and its top end is secured to a "strong point" in the aircraft. The length of the static line is twelve feet six inches. The strop has to be long enough to ensure that the parachute will be well below the aircraft before it opens, and short enough so that the chute is not caught in the slipstream and twisted round the rear plane or the tail-wheel. In a Dakota the strop is attached to a steel cable running along the side of the aircraft. The strop attachment is clipped to this cable and moves with the jumpers as they shuffle one by one towards the exit.

The canopy of the parachute is usually made of nylon, though sometimes of cotton, and has a diameter of twenty-eight feet. In the middle of it is a circular hole, the vent, twenty-two inches in diameter. This vent prevents undue strain on the canopy when it begins to open and is said to reduce oscillation. The rigging lines attaching the canopy to the harness are twenty-two feet long. When not in use the parachute reposes in its bag, put there by an expert packer. About twenty-five minutes are needed to inspect and pack a parachute. It must not remain longer than two months in its bag nor must it be used for more than twenty-five descents. The packers, for the most part women belonging to the Women's Auxiliary Air Force, perform a highly skilled and vital service. The fact that the failure of the canopy to open is the rarest cause, of such rare accidents as occur, is proof of their efficiency. The parachutist relies on them implicitly.

A nibbling feeling at the shoulders

The signal to jump is first a warning red light and then a green, after which the parachutists jump one after the other with the utmost rapidity. The object, which is not at all easy to attain, is for each man to fall in as small an area as possible, and they are dropped in sticks of ten or more, immediately before the moment of dropping, the pilot of the aircraft will throttle back so as to fly as slowly as possible without stalling. The maximum ideal speed is not more than one hundred miles an hour, but jumps are frequently made from aircraft travelling at least one-third as fast again, and sometimes even faster.

Once outside in the blue or grey air, the parachute soldier falls from one to one-and-a-half seconds before, first the strop, which pulls out the static line in the top half of the inner bag, and then the line itself, which pulls out the parachute from the bottom half, become taut. When these two operations have occurred, the canopy of the parachute develops, the headlong fall is checked, and the jumper begins to float towards the earth. "On falling through the hole," says one who has jumped many times, "your legs are immediately blown into a, horizontal position by the slipstream and you find yourself parallel to the ground. A moment later there is a nibbling feeling at your shoulders. The canopy is opened, but the jerk is no harder than that made by a fair-sized trout when you hook it. After that all sensation of falling ends." Some parachutists would maintain that the jerk is more abrupt ; all agree that the opening of the canopy produces a sound like the crack of a whip.

Though seeming to fall but slowly, the jumper is, in fact, approaching the earth considerably faster than he appears to be. Moreover, since he is moving through the air, it is hard for him to gauge with exactness the precise moment at which he will strike the earth. The shock may be compared with that experienced by jumping blindfold from a height of from six to eight feet.

More than one danger or difficulty may beset the parachute soldier when he is still in the air or immediately after he has touched the ground. The rigging lines of the parachute may become twisted. He may have made a faulty exit and somersaulted, thus becoming entangled in the rigging lines.

The parachute itself may begin to oscillate till the jumper is swinging like the ball or disc on the end of a pendulum. This swing was one of the reasons why leaping from the rear end of a Whitley was abandoned. When the canopy opened, the jumper was blown at once into a horizontal position and thus began the descent by swinging violently, and the swing was sometimes not ended by the time he had touched earth. All these troubles and difficulties can be corrected in the air, provided that the parachute soldier knows his drill and keeps his head. His greatest difficulty is to strike the ground without injury. "The landing is usually considered the main problem in parachuting. It is certainly the most interesting," remarks the Parachute Training Manual somewhat drily. It goes on : "If a landing is made correctly, injury even in rough weather is almost unknown, but, if made incorrectly, it is more than probable."

No foolproof method has yet been evolved to achieve the two main objects, which are to absorb the shock of the impact by distributing it all over the body, and to touch down in such a way as to make certain that only those parts of the body best suited for the purpose should act as the points of shock absorption. Parachute soldiers are taught to flex the ankles, the knees, the hips and then the back, immediately on touching the ground. These actions become almost automatic, and this applies to the next phase which is to roll so that the shock is absorbed by, if possible, the whole or the greater part of the body.

One point is of supreme importance. The legs must be kept together, and the soles of the feet as nearly as possible parallel to the ground, so that both feet may touch the earth simultaneously. Once safely landed, the parachute soldier operates his quick-release gear, frees himself of his parachute and its harness, and moves off to the rendezvous previously chosen.

Captain W. P. B. Bradish, one of the first instructors, was considered to be far advanced in the art of parachuting after he had jumped a number of times through a hole in a mock fuselage on to a mat six feet below ; but, as soon as the training syllabus had been worked out and put into operation, six and then ten jumps had to be made, one of them by night, before the soldier could wear on his right upper arm the wings joined by a parachute - the badge of the trained parachutist.

Common sense, determination, will-power

Such, very briefly, are sonic of the problems which face the parachute soldier and which he learns to overcome by drill and training. But, and this is a point to be remembered-the knowledge imparted to the parachute troops who dropped in North Africa in 1942; in Sicily in 1943, in Normandy and Holland in 1944, and in Germany in 1945, and which enabled them to play so important a part in the military operations then and there conducted, had been acquired at the Central Landing Establishment by that small band of single-minded officers and other ranks of the Army and the Royal Air Force chosen to fulfil the instructions of the Prime Minister. Laboriously and at the risk of broken limbs and lost lives, a risk that sometimes became a reality, they acquired a skill and technique which they imparted to willing, and nearly always successful, pupils.

These, as has been said, were all volunteers. Only a very few of the applicants were accepted, and at first hardly any of them showed any fear of jumping. It was a new adventure, and these men, being young, were adventurous. Moreover, their country was fighting a desperate war of which the end could only be annihilation or victory. From the very beginning it was borne in upon them that it would be their proud lot to be in the forefront in preventing the first and achieving the second. Their calling, therefore, set them, to a certain extent, apart from their fellow men, even from their comrades in their own and the other two Services. Like the Commandos, they were allowed in a special manner to use those qualities of individual courage and intelligence which distinguishes the able fighting man from the ordinary man-in-the-street turned soldier. Yet it must not be supposed that the early volunteers, or indeed those who followed them, were of some special breed. They were not. Experience soon showed that common sense and character were the main ingredients of the successful parachute trooper, and these qualities are not rare. One ability he had to possess-sufficient strength of will to conquer doubt and fear. Though, as statistics prove, the number of accidents as compared with the number of drops is infinitesimal, yet he who will cast himself into the void from a hole in the floor or from a doorway in the side of a noisy, swiftly moving and not always steady machine, must be endowed with certain qualities not in the possession of every man, or, more accurately, he must possess those qualities in a greater degree of intensity. Under the impulse of necessity most of us would probably jump once with a parachute on our backs, but those of us who would make a practice of so doing are not so numerous. Thus determination and will-power are two essential attributes of the parachute soldier.

Before long it became clear that recruits unable to withstand the emotional strain inseparable from their 'new calling were unsuitable, though it was necessary to make a clear distinction between those who refused to jump because of an abnormal fear of height or of flying, and those who lacked the moral stamina to do so. It was soon found that if a pupil refused to jump he would probably never be able to overcome this disability and that to give him a second chance was therefore a mistake. Cajolery and persuasion were discovered to be no part of an instructor's moral armoury. All that was necessary was the ability to give normal encouragement. In this the instructors at the Central Landing Establishment have been aided not a little by two ladies, Mrs. Stokes and Mrs. Smalley, and their band of helpers, who for more than three years have provided hot drinks, food and cigarettes at all hours of the day and night from two Y.M.C.A. canteens to men undergoing a period of undoubted, though often unconscious, strain.

Physically, a light, short man, provided he possesses sufficient strength and stamina, is preferred as a parachute soldier to a taller, heavier man ; but tall or short, broad or slim, all must possess a very high degree of physical fitness. `

The parachute soldier, then, must be of high quality both in mind and body. That he is so, the actions in which he fought in this war amply prove. Though with the strange modesty of the Englishman he would in all probability claim to be not in the least remarkable, yet the fact remains that the very nature of his duties makes him of that splendid company to be found in all the Services who may properly be described as the élite of the nation. All good troops take a proper pride in their achievements and the skill which makes them possible; but the parachute soldier always remembers that pride comes after, not before, a fall.

Training Devices

At first training at the School progressed but slowly, mainly for lack of aircraft. Since Whitleys were not available in any number, a system of "synthetic" ground training was evolved, of which the object was to simulate in the hangar, by means of various kinds of apparatus, conditions which would be met in the air. A number of curious-looking machines were constructed, of which the strangest and least appreciated was an apparatus soon known by the sinister nickname of "The Gallows." The jumper, suspended in his harness from one end of a rope, jumped through an aperture till his descent was abruptly checked by a weight at the other end of the rope corresponding to within a few pounds with his own. It was hoped and believed that this could simulate very accurately the shock of alighting ; but sprains, twisted ankles and dislocated knees soon showed that the calculations of its inventor were not entirely accurate, and its use was presently abandoned, as was also the practice of leaping from moving lorries, which too often caused similar injuries.

Such devices and habits belonged to a period when experiment had to go hand in hand with training. It was Wing Commander J. C. Kilkenny, O.B.E., who has been Chief Instructor at the Parachute Training School for nearly four years, who evolved and perfected a system which, though it be like all good systems subject to improvement, has withstood exacting tests and is now the standard method in daily use.

It is designed to teach the pupil on the ground the actions he must subsequently perform when jumping from an aircraft, when falling' through the air and when landing. For this purpose two hangars have been converted into gymnasia of unconventional aspect. In the first are fuselages of all the types of aircraft used and "mock-ups" of their doors and apertures. In the second are to be found a number of appliances resembling trapezes, swings and those wooden chutes down which the frequenters of fun-fairs delight to slide. The most ingenious is, perhaps, the device known as the "Fan." A steel cable wound about a drum is connected to a parachute harness. Wearing it the jumper leaps from a platform twenty-five feet above the floor. The weight of his body as he falls causes the drum to revolve, but its speed, as the cable pays out, is checked by two vanes or fans which revolve with it and thus create an air-brake. The pupil first learns how to cast himself through the various apertures and doors of the fuselages in the first hangar and then spends many hours of practice on the appliances in the second.

Each Sergeant-Instructor is in charge of a "stick" of ten, and eight or nine sticks form a syndicate under an Officer Instructor. The course lasts from two to three weeks, according to the weather, and, during that time, except when engaged on jumping from a balloon or an aircraft, the pupil spends his time in the hangars hard at work under the energetic and enthusiastic direction of such men as Sergeant Walsh, once a bus conductor, Flight Sergeant Smallfield, once a seaman, Sergeant Cleaver, once a licensed victualler, or Sergeant Eckersley, once a drum-maker, and many others who have left their varied civil occupations to train young and vigorous volunteers in a young and vigorous method of entry into battle. Comprehensive and exact statistical records are maintained, the most important being those relating to injuries. Unceasing care has reduced these to very small proportions, and those of a serious nature scarcely exceed one-third of one per cent.

Little by little the numbers of trained men increased. Up to August 1941 the training capacity of the parachute-dropping squadron was forty parachutists a week. After that month it increased to a hundred. In September of that year, 1,365 drops were made from aircraft, and in December this figure increased to over 4,000. It is now many times greater.

Aircraft being scarce, practice drops had to be made from captive balloons, a form of experience by no means entirely pleasant. On November 27th, 1940, three instructors travelled to Henlow and thence to Cardington, the home before the war of the ill-fated R type of airship, where they were confronted by an elderly balloon moored to the floor of the largest shed. "A less secure-looking apparatus," reported Captain J. R. Elliott, "from which to make a parachute descent it would be difficult to find. The fabric was patched and mended ; the fins flapped lazily like elephants' ears ; and the car was nothing more than a big matchbox with the top cut away." The balloon had once been silver-grey in colour, "but the birds had changed all that." Since the wind blowing across the airfield outside was too high, no jump was attempted that day and the three men made instead an ascent which took place inside the shed. It was an uncomfortable experience.

The envelope bumped and bounced against the roof, disturbing the bats and pigeons which had their homes there. The three instructors crouched uneasily in the car. Presently "Brereton got to his feet, looked over the side and was sick. Ward raised himself slowly, looked over the side and was sick. I was sick." The next day was calm, and it was decided to attempt a descent on to the airfield. This was successfully accomplished in the afternoon, and the possibilities of using balloons in parachute training were proved.

More balloons were later provided by the Air Ministry, and it presently became the practice for the first two drops of the recruit to be made from the car of a captive balloon. This method of jumping has a further advantage, for it enables the instructor on the ground beneath to direct and control the movements of his pupil in the air by means of a loudspeaker.

Weapons from the air

Another problem of great though more technical importance was how to arm the parachute soldier-to supply him with weapons and ammunition so that he would be in a position tonight unaided by the regular supply services until such time as the army on the ground had made contact with him. There is a limit to what can be carried by a man descending by parachute. How great it was had to be discovered. A container was designed, a rifle and "a bag of shot" loaded into it, and it was then dropped from a height of 800 feet. "The thing worked in principle," Rock records in his war diary, "but the rifle and shot came through the bottom of the container. We sent it back with remarks." After a time bigger and better containers were designed and constructed, so that it eventually became possible to drop Bren guns, two-inch mortars, and ammunition quite safely by these means. In 1942 Major Lander, who by then had had two years' operational experience, devised a method of dropping with as much as 100 lb. weight of extra supplies attached to the parachutist. The ammunition or machine-gun was put in a bag attached to one end of seventy feet of rope, the other end being secured to the jumper's waist. After leaving the aircraft, the bag was allowed to fall the full length of the rope, thus increasing the speed of descent. The bag, being below the jumper, was the first to strike the ground ; its weight was thus neutralized, the speed of descent of the parachutist was checked, and he could land safely. This "kit-bag" method of carrying arms and supplies has supplanted to a considerable extent the use of containers, which are often hard to find, especially in close country.

These and other experiments were constantly made by men whose training and whose task caused them to leave nothing to chance. They were engaged in perfecting a new way to bring that most senior of all Warriors, the infantry soldier, into swift and close contact with the enemy.

CHAPTER 3
THE GLIDER AND ITS TUG

URING THE MONTH of September 1940 an order was placed by the Ministry of Aircraft Production for 400 Hotspur gliders. The Hotspur was the prototype of the operational Horsas and Hamilcars which were to follow in due course.

Progress was very slow, for the aircraft industry was engaged in producing bombers and lighters in an unending effort to keep pace with the unending demands of the Royal Air Force. It was not until well on into 1942 that the Horsa glider became available, in slowly increasing quantities. In its final form the Horsa is a high-winged monoplane with a tricycle undercarriage which can be jettisoned if need be in favour of a central skid. Its overall length is 67 feet, its span 88 feet, and the height to the top of the large fin to which the rudder is attached is nineteen feet six inches.

Inside, the Horsa looks not unlike a section of the London Tube railway in miniature, the fuselage being circular and made of a skin of plywood attached to numerous circular ribs of stouter wood. The seats run down the length of each side and are also of light wood, each being provided with a safety harness fitting over the shoulders of the wearer, while a belt encircles his waist. The floor of the glider is corrugated to prevent slipping. There are two entrances, one to port near the nose, the other to starboard near the stern. The doors slide vertically upwards, but the whole tail unit is detachable to enable the quick unloading of jeeps, anti-tank guns and other heavy material. In an emergency the tail can be blown off by means of a dynamite cartridge, but this method involves a risk of tire. Escape hatches are fitted so that, if the glider falls into the sea, the occupants can leave it quickly.

One great advantage possessed by gliders is that their wooden construction gives them buoyancy. Some of them have been known to float for twenty-four hours.

The angle of dangle

The two pilots sit side by side, the first pilot being on the left. The controls are similar to those of a power-driven aircraft except that there are no throttles. Instead, a small lever, painted red, operates the tow-rope release.

One instrument, fitted fairly recently, is of special importance, for by means of it the glider pilot can fly correctly at night or in cloud when he cannot see the tug. It is the Cable Angle Indicator, known colloquially as the " Angle of Dangle " and consists of two illuminated white lines on the face of a dial, one horizontal, the other vertical. These are connected with the tow rope, whose slightest movements cause them also to move. By keeping his eye on them, the pilot knows when the tug is in the correct position and can take immediate action to remedy a fault in flying. The correct position to be assumed by the glider is either slightly above the tug, high-tow, or slightly below it, low-tow. The glider must never be directly behind the tug, for the slipstream would cause it to oscillate so violently that the tow rope would soon snap. The breaking of the tow rope is naturally the chief fear of the pilot, and it may assume the proportions of a nightmare if he is flying in cloudy and bumpy weather. The strength of the rope depends on the strength of the tug's fuselage and the nose of the glider, to which it is attached by a simple bolt-and-shackle device. Too strong a rope would mean putting too great a strain on the tug ; too weak would lead to frequent snapping.

For the Horsa the circumference of the tow rope is 35g inches, for its larger freight-carrying brother, the Hamilcar, 4.2 inches.

The rope is waterproof, 350 feet long, and contains within it the telephone wires connecting the pilot of the glider with the pilot of the tug.

The Hamilcar is considerably larger than the Horsa and is used to carry freight only. This may consist of a light tank or two Bren-gun carriers, or two jeeps with trailers. They are all carried in the front half of the glider, of which the interior resembles a long rectangular barn tapering towards the stern, and looking not unlike a distended, four-sided concertina. Two tracks to carry the vehicles run from the nose to a point about half-way down the glider, and on these they stand, being shackled to various strong points by cables and chains. The nose of the Hamilcar is hinged so that it can open like a door, and since the vehicles are housed in the forepart, their weight causes the glider to tip up on being brought to a standstill and thus they can run straight out on to the ground without making use of a ramp.

The crews of all vehicles remain in them throughout the trip, and when nearing the ground the engines are started so that the jeep or carrier can be driven away the instant the nose is swung back.

Both the Horsa and the Hamilcar are fitted with large flaps, which enable them to be dived at a comparatively steep angle and thus, if necessary, brought quickly to the ground after being cast off. The landing speed in still air is not less than 70 m.p.h.No glider pilot or glider-borne soldier carries a parachute, but all wear Mae Wests.

The first glider exercises

In 1940 and 1941 such gliders as these and troop-carriers such as the Stirling and the Halifax, were still an aim, not an accomplishment. Through those first difficult eighteen months Rock, Norman, Newnham and the rest laboured unceasingly at their task. Their mood was sometimes grim, for those early days of experiment were difficult and rendered more so by lack of equipment and aircraft. The first parachute exercise took place on December 3rd, 1940, in the presence of the then Commander-in-Chief, Home Forces. By that date some 350 parachute soldiers had made single jumps, and the technique of jumping in " sticks " was being developed. On this occasion the dropping zone was bounded on one side by a railway and on the other by some high-tension cables. It was a foggy morning but the mist cleared, and at a minute before nine o'clock the first of the four Whitleys taking part appeared. The drops were made without incident and included the dropping of a container distinguishable by the red parachute to which it was attached. On reaching the ground the parachutists, all save one, who had dislocated his -knee-cap, formed up and made for their objective, encountering on the way the motor car of the Crown Prince Olaf of Norway.

Putting one of the lessons they had been taught into immediate practice, they commandeered it and its driver and thus reached their objective, a nearby airfield, all the faster.

The first glider exercise was a modest one, and those who witnessed it must have required no little imagination to picture the huge fleets of huge gliders belonging to the types just described, which only four years later were seen by the battered and triumphant inhabitants of Britain on the wing for the Netherlands and the Rhine. On an autumn day, October 26th, 1940, two single-seater sail planes moved slowly by behind two Avro 504 tugs.

Six months later it was possible to stage a well-combined exercise for the benefit of the Prime Minister. It was no more than a demonstration. On April 26th, 1941, a formation of six Whitleys dropped their full complement of parachute soldiers, five sail planes landed in formation, and one Hotspur was towed past the visitor. By then it had been realized that to train 5,000 airborne soldiers was a task requiring a great deal of time. Soon after this demonstration a Glider Exercise Unit was formed, and the technical and tactical problems connected with the use of gliders were worked out by Rock and Wing Commander P. B. N. Davis. It was then that the foundations of what is now the general practice were laid. Expansion continued, and the number of glider-training units considerably increased, until they occupied several stations of the R.A.F.

By November 1941 the initial period of experiment was drawing to a close.

The foundations had been laid strongly and well. Now at last the house could be built. In that month Major-General F. A. M. Browning, C.B.E., D.S.O., M.C., was appointed General Officer Commanding Airborne Forces and provided with a skeleton staff. From that time on, despite a multitude of difficulties and disappointments, there was no looking back. Airborne Forces were now an integral part of the British Army and presently wore on their heads the maroon-coloured beret soon to become famous and on their shoulders Bellerophon astride winged Pegasus.

"Right adjuncts of the war"

Browning and his staff began working in underground offices in Whitehall, which earned for them the nickname of "The Dungeon Party." From these holes deep in the ground, schemes to take troops high in the air to the battlefield were thought out and perfected. The first parachute brigade under Brigadier (now Major-General) R. N. Gale, D.S.O., O.B.E., M.C., was formed at that time, shortly to be followed by the first air landing brigade under Brigadier G. F. Hopkinson, O.B.E., M.C. Browning is a Guardsman and therefore knows the supreme value in war of highly trained, well-disciplined troops. The first parachutists had been of the guerrilla type, and not a few of them had seen service in the Spanish Civil War, some on one side, some on another. They were formed into troops of fifty, composed of a captain, two subalterns and forty-seven other ranks. The officers were responsible for the ground training, and great latitude had been allowed.

It is no more possible to deny that this was necessary in the early stages of development than it is to question the work of Lieutenant-Colonel E. E. Down, C.B.E., who adopted more regular methods. Under him and his successors the parachutists learnt a way of life and acquired a standard of discipline equal to the highest in the Army. The selection and early training took place, and still does, at the Airborne Forces School and Depot." Here is decided the rejection of unsuitable candidates and here those who survive the first tests are put through a preliminary course of rigorous training under Army, Instructors. This Depot is to the Airborne Forces what Caterham is to the Brigade of Guards, a place of trial but not of error.

One problem engaged the special attention of those in command. It was how to keep parachute soldiers in good form so that they should not lose their initial keenness or become oppressed by the daily uncertainty of the immediate future. Seldom could the day and hour be prophesied when a jump would be made. The Whitleys might be unserviceable ; the weather might be unsuitable ; these and other factors impossible to foresee made much waiting inevitable. However enthusiastic and strong-minded a man may be, such waiting is a strain on his nerves, and every effort was made to palliate or remove its possible danger. From the very first it had been recognised and unceasingly proclaimed to those concerned that to drop by parachute or to land from a glider was but a quick and novel way of reaching the battlefield. It was no more than this. Because a man landed successfully, he was not necessarily a good soldier. One of the first lessons, therefore, which had to be taught and assimilated was that this form of reaching the battlefield was merely incidental, a means whereby a highly trained soldier could be taken to a spot where he could inflict the greatest hurt on the enemy.

Very detailed and comprehensive programmes of infantry

training were, therefore, instituted and carried out by all recruits to airborne forces. They were already trained soldiers when they reached the Central Landing Establishment. There, until the Depot was established, their training continued and was intensified, the art of dropping being merely an incident in the prescribed course. Thus the period of waiting was filled with strenuous military exercises and even more strenuous physical training, but both might be interrupted for an hour or so at any moment by an order which sent the platoon into the waiting Whitley and thence by parachute on to some nearby airfield. When, in addition to parachute troops, battalions of glider-borne infantry began to be formed, a development which did not assume any large proportions until after the Allied landing in North Africa in the late autumn of 1942-the same principles were followed, The aim was in each case the same-to train a body of already highly competent infantry soldiers to the highest possible pitch.

From the start it was decided that it would be waste of time and energy to take less well qualified troops to battle by these expensive means. Expensive in every sense. A parachute or a glider can rarely be used on operations more than once and—far more important-their use for the conveying of troops to the scene of conflict involves, as will be seen, meticulous planning and considerable effort on the part of the Royal Air Force. This is altogether justifiable if the troops are worth their salt, but not otherwise. Thus it is that airborne soldiers have from the outset been required to reach the very highest standard. To them more than to any other branch of the Army can the words, mutatis mutandis, of Tamburlaine to his sons be applied :

"I'll have you learn to sleep upon the ground,
March in your armour through the watery fens,
Sustain the scorching heat and freezing cold,
Hunger and thirst, right adjuncts of the war,
And after this to scale a castle wall,

Besiege a fort, to undermine a town,
And make whole cities caper in the air."

The Glider Pilot Regiment is formed

Half and presently more than half of General Browning's Command consisted of airborne troops carried to battle in gliders. A Glider Pilot Regiment, for it had been decided that the pilots should belong to the Army was therefore formed by Rock in January 1942, and he himself went to a Training School with forty Army officers and other ranks in order to learn the business of flying gliders, While he was away, Major (now Brigadier) George Chatterton, D.S.O., was given the task of raising the regiment. To do so was no easy matter. That there were a large number of enthusiastic volunteers available was most fortunate, but what they were to be trained to do beyond flying a glider had not been fully determined. Rock and Chatterton set to work, and in a short time produced a Directive on the air and military training of glider pilots, much of it based on the views of Rock, Davis and Nigel Norman. There was one cardinal principle which was regarded as essential, and which has from the very beginning imbued each and every man of the Glider Regiment. It was that the glider pilot must be a " total " soldier. Not only must he be able to fly with the utmost skill and resolution ; he must also be equally at home manning a Bren gun after landing, or driving a jeep, or tiring a rifle, an anti-tank gun, or a mortar.

He must be at once a jack-of-all-trades and a master of each.

Glider pilots had to reach as high a standard on the ground as they attained in the air. How they conducted themselves in North Africa, Sicily, Normandy, Holland and the Rhine shows with .what fortitude and unanimity it was reached. Their bearing on every field of battle ennobled by their presence has been that of soldiers determined to maintain and further the highest traditions of the British Army, having already in the air lived up to those of the Royal Air Force. Captain W. N. Barrie, D.F.C., who after having flown 450 miles to Sicily, landed his six-pounder anti-tank gun and fought it for three days ; or Sergeant Pilot Galpin who, released at 6,000 feet six miles from Syracuse, glided through flak and searchlights to land by the all-important bridge whose capture was essential to success, and there fought as a Bren-gunner for seventeen hours ; or Sergeant Pilot Ainsworth who, falling into the sea off Sicily, swam with a wounded man, towing him for two miles to shore, killed two sentries with a knife, his only weapon, and disarmed another, captured twenty prisoners, fought as an infantryman for several days, and a year later flew as second pilot in the glider which landed next the swing bridge over the Caen Canal, are but three examples chosen at random of what these men, who wear the wings joined by a crown surmounted by a lion's head, can and do accomplish in the course of duty.

They first went into action on November 19th, 1942.

Out of the many thousand volunteers interviewed for the purpose of choosing glider pilots, only very few were accepted. Of these, a third failed to pass their qualifying tests or to reach the military standard required. It is thus only a chosen band who have been judged worthy to follow this arduous and gallant calling. As with the parachute soldier, they represent every regiment in the British Army.

There are also the aircraft and pilots of the Royal Air Force to be considered. Here again much trouble was experienced. Harvey and Norman, both indefatigable, worked with a grim energy to fulfil their task in the teeth of difficulties of every kind. The War Office and the Air Ministry, their joint masters, were for months greatly occupied with problems which seemed to them, and indeed were, more urgent than the training of airborne troops to be used only when Great Britain switched from defence to attack.

As far back as June 10th, 1940, a conference of experts in the Air Ministry had decided that the Whitley was the only aircraft suitable for the carriage of parachute soldiers, the reason being that it had a turret situated on the underside of the fuselage which could be fairly easily removed, the resulting void being used as the jumping hole. Eleven days after this conference, four Whitleys were detailed to form the nucleus of the air transport side of the Central Landing Establishment, and for a long time they remained a nucleus, little or nothing being added to them.

The aircraft and the crews

When gliders came into use it was necessary to decide by what type of aircraft they should be towed. It had to be one with a reserve of power or its engines would overheat. Once again the Whitley was pressed into service ; other aircraft detailed for towing were the Hector, the Master and, later on, the Albemarle, Halifax, Stirling and Dakota. For a long time Hectors and Masters towed Hotspurs, but they were quite unable to deal with the larger Horsa. In June 1942 a decision was made to allocate the Albemarle, a fairly fast medium bomber with a tricycle undercarriage, for use as a troop-carrier or a tug. Much good experimental work was carried out using this aircraft for towing at a time when nothing else was suitable or available. Albemarles were used in the Sicilian operations in July 1943. They were succeeded by Dakotas, Halifaxes and Stirlings.

The crew of a tug have to be as highly trained as those of a bomber, and it took some little time for this to be brought home. Moreover, in the early days, trained crews as well as aircraft were needed for immediate operations against the enemy. Nevertheless a few were forthcoming at the start, and their numbers had grown by February 1942, when Army Co-operation Command formed No. 38 Wing to provide the transport necessary for air-borne forces. At the outset it possessed only eight trained crews. Eighty-six Blenheim crews, of whom forty-live had reached the necessary operational standard, were hastily drafted to the Wing, of which Norman was the first commander;

but some time elapsed before the full complement of aircraft and crews were available for operations.

During all those weary months of unending training and very few operations, something of great importance was learnt. It was that the tug and the glider must be not only a physical, but a mental and moral, combination ; in other words, only the closest feeling of comradeship between the crew in the first and the pilots in the second could achieve the high standard of efficiency required. That this lesson took some time to learn was due, not so much to the reluctance of both parties, as to the fact that for many months they were separated by a considerable distance. By the autumn of 1942 some hundreds of glider pilots had been trained and were in Army camps on Salisbury Plain. An adequate supply of gliders and tugs was not available, however, to keep them in training, with the inevitable result not only that the pilots became out of practice, but also that they could have no contact with the crews of the tugs. Such a state of affairs was presently remedied, but it took time to do so.

The problem of keeping in good heart the crews of the aircraft engaged in carrying parachutists or towing tugs was faced from the outset and solved by Nigel Norman. No. 38 Wing was allowed from time to time to send aircraft to take part in bombing and other operations against the enemy. The targets chosen for them were in every case those of a type which might one day be attacked by parachute troops. They were Transformer Stations, to hit which it is necessary to fly low and bomb with great accuracy. Objectives of this kind near Chartres and between Le Mans and Paris were attacked with considerable success, though the loss on one such operation of three aircraft out of the ten dispatched was relatively high.

Other operations included the dropping of men and supplies to those persons in France and other countries who had never accepted the dominion of the Germans and were fighting them with every means in their power.

The number of these patriots grew steadily as the war progressed, and their appetite for arms and ammunition was insatiable. To assuage it was difficult at first, and even towards the end the supplies dropped, great though they were, never equalled the demand. Such operations provided at once excellent training for our crews and an opportunity, constantly renewed, of keeping them up to the mark. Many hundreds of missions to districts as far distant as the Savoy Alps and the Pyrenees were made by pilots and crews under training with the airborne forces. The performance of such duties caused the navigators of the airborne Wing to be numbered among the most skilful of the Royal Air Force. As time went on and the instruments were invented and perfected, increasing use was made of Radar navigational devices. They added greatly to the skill of navigators. A third advantage of carrying out bombing and supply-dropping operations was to accustom the crews to anti-aircraft tire. This was known as " flak inoculation " and proved invaluable in giving pilots that measure of steadiness and cold determination which enabled them to fly a straight course to the dropping and landing zones.

Thus did all branches of airborne troops-the parachutists, the glider pilots, the glider-borne infantry and the Royal Air Force crews-train through long months during which it seemed that it would never be their lot to take part in any operation on a large scale. Yet all the time they were becoming steadily more and more skilled and more and more tit to wage a most novel and hazardous form of warfare.

As has been explained, the airborne forces are composed partly of parachute troops and partly of glider-borne. Both are organised in battalions and brigades, and together they form airborne divisions. Those who go to war in gliders, the Air Landing Brigades, differ from their parachutist comrades in one important respect. Some but by no means all are volunteers, the original members of certain regiments of the Line. At the beginning their ranks were comprised either of Regular or Territorial soldiers. The gaps caused by casualties have been filled by those called to the colours through the operation of the National Service Acts. Many of the troops composing an airborne division belong to it not from choice but as the result of orders, yet the behaviour of these men on the field of battle leaves no doubt as to the wisdom of such a decision. They have most worthily upheld old and honourable traditions and have added fresh lustre to regimental colours blazoned with the names of battles fought when Marlborough and Wellington were the general officers in command.

The airborne divisions are carried to battle by aircraft of the Royal Air Force. Several Wings now operate, and were under the command of Air Vice-Marshal Hollinghurst, whose place was taken by the late Air Vice-Marshal Scarlett-Streatfield in the Autumn of 1944.

The moment has now come to describe the exploits of these troops, from the first small beginning on February 10th, 1941, when a party of parachutists dropped from six Whitleys near an aqueduct in southern Italy with intent to destroy it, to March 24th, 1945, when two divisions, one British and one American, took the air against an enemy keeping a sullen, and as it turned out, wholly inadequate watch on the Rhine.

CHAPTER 4

PRELIMINARY BOUTS: MONTE VULTURE AND BRUNEVAL

ABOUT THIRTY MILES east-north-east of the little town of Salverno in the province of Campagna, which is in the ankle of Italy, an aqueduct crosses a small stream, the Tragino. It is the main water supply for all the province of Apulia, 'in which at that time a population of some two million Italians lived, for the most part in Taranto, Brindisi, Bari, Foggia and other towns.

Most of them were workers in factories, dockyards, and other places of military importance. To deprive them for a month of their regular water supply and force them to depend on local reservoirs would, it was hoped, create a degree of confusion and dislocation which might have a serious, possibly even a vital, effect on the two campaigns then being waged by Mussolini, the one in North Africa, the other in Albania. A London firm of engineers suggested this target and provided a number of details concerning it.

To bomb with the certainty of hitting it was very difficult, if not impossible, for the modern type of bombsight and the other instruments of precision now in use were not then available. It was therefore decided that it should be attacked by a force of parachutists carrying explosives powerful enough to destroy at least one of the main pillars supporting the aqueduct.

This operation and the next, against the radiolocation post at Bruneval, have already been described in an official book, Combined Operations, but an account of the exploits of airborne forces would be incomplete without some reference to them, since it was these forces which carried them out.

Moreover, certain new facts are now available.

On January 24th, 1941, Lieutenant A. J. Deane-Drummond, M.C., was ordered to Malta in a Sunderland to make all preparations for the raid, which was to start from that island. In the meantime fifty officers and other ranks from No. 11 Air Service Battalion were detailed for the expedition. When it became known in the Central Landing Establishment that action of some kind against the enemy was contemplated, a long queue of parachute soldiers formed outside the orderly room, each man ready with some ingenious reason to prove that he at least was indispensable to its success. Eventually the numbers were reduced to seven officers and thirty-one other ranks, of whom two were Italian anti-Fascists burning to serve the true cause of their country. They were to act as interpreters. This small force was under the command of Major T. A. C. Pritchard, and was composed partly of Royal Engineers whose duty it would be to blow up the aqueduct- these were under the command of Captain G. F. K. Daly- and partly of infantry who would form the covering party.

They rehearsed for some three weeks under the energetic supervision of Rock, while six Whitleys were prepared for the operation. Two more were to take part in it and to create a diversion by bombing the railway yard at Foggia.

Moonlight, snow, and an aqueduct

At dusk on February 7th, 1941, the Whitleys took off, arriving safely the next day at Malta with their freight of parachutists after a flight of nearly 1,600 miles. On the next day Flying Officer A. Warburton, D.S.O., D.F.C., landed with photographs of the objective taken that morning. It lay south-west of Monte Vulture "in wild and desolate country," and the pictures showed not one but two aqueducts clearly outlined against a snow-covered background. The second ran 200 yards to the west of the first which was the larger of the two and was therefore singled out for attack. By then, His Majesty's submarine "Triumph" had received orders to be off the mouth of the river Sele by the night of February 15th/16th, ready to embark the returning parachutists, who were to make their way thither on foot.

At dusk on February 10th the eight Whitleys took off from Malta, six of them with the parachutists on board and two with bombs. In one of these Nigel Norman was flying. Neither he nor Rock had been allowed to take a more active part in the expedition ; their value as instructors was too great. The first of the six Whitleys was due over the target at 9.30 p.m. It arrived at 9.42, flying at 400 feet, and dropped its load of men and containers from 50 up to 250 yards from the target. The others followed suit, but their drop was not quite so accurate, the farthest man landing three-quarters of a mile away. A few landed in a dry river bed. So far, all had gone well, but the sixth Whitley had lost its way. It eventually arrived in the area three quarters of an hour late and slightly off course. The parachutists it contained were in consequence dropped, not near the objective, but in the next valley, too far away to take any part in the action. This was unfortunate, for they consisted of Daly and his engineers.

Weather conditions were excellent. It was bright moonlight and the aqueduct was clearly seen. Pritchard, Deane-Drummond, and Second Lieutenant G. W. Paterson, set about collecting the containers, a task of some difficulty for they were scattered and the lights on some of them were not shining. To help them, the parachutists called upon twelve of the local inhabitants from a farmhouse nearby. Docile and obedient, these Italian hinds trudged off to their task, one of them remarking that nothing ever happened in that part of the world and that he would now have enough to talk' about for the rest of his life.

In the absence of Daly, Pritchard ordered Paterson and such sappers as were with him to carry out the demolition, protected by the covering party under the command of Deane-Drummond, who had discovered a track which crossed the Genestra, a small stream near by, by means of a rough bridge close to some farm buildings. On examining the pier, Paterson found that it was made, not of masonry as he had been led to expect, but of concrete, a substance more difficult to break. He concentrated all the quantity of explosive available-it was not as great as it might have been, for, owing to icing, two containers had failed to leave the aircraft-against the westernmost pier and its abutment. Six hundred and forty pounds of explosives were put against the first and 160 against the second. Lance-Corporal Watson put the charges in position and all was ready soon after midnight. By then the Italian peasants who had collected the containers had been shepherded into the farm buildings near the small bridge, and some of them tied up.

They were warned by one of the interpreters that if they attempted to leave the house they would be shot, and that a sentry with these orders was outside the door. In point of fact no sentry had been posted- the threat sufficed.

At 12.30 a.m. the main charge was fired. A moment later the small bridge discovered by Deane-Drummond went up, large pieces of it crashing on the roof of the farmhouse, but hurting no one. Pritchard and Paterson examined the pier, found that it had collapsed, that the waterway it supported had been broken in two, and that the water was beginning to flood the ravine.

"No choice but to surrender"

It was time to make for the submarine. The parachutists formed up, all save one who had broken a leg on landing and was left behind in the farmhouse in the care of the farmer. They threw away their heavy equipment and started off in three parties to cover the fifty miles separating them from the mouth of the river Sele. It was then about one o'clock in the morning of February 11th and they had to reach their destination by the night of the 15th/16th. Revolvers were carried, and one Thompson sub-machine gun for each party. Pritchard led the way up a mountain till the snow line was reached. This they skirted till they found a small wooded valley, where they lay up for the day, being fearful that some children playing near by might discover and betray them. When darkness had fallen they started off again, following the flank of the mountains and crossing the Sele undetected by means of a bridge. When dawn broke they hoped to hide in a wood shown on their maps as crowning the summit of the Cresta di Gallo- in English, the Cock 's comb. They pushed on higher and higher through the cold darkness until they found themselves walking in the snow of the mountain. By now dawn was in the sky and no wood was to be seen. They looked round for cover. Some of them found it in a small cave near the top of the Cock 's comb, others behind the rocks and tree-stumps which strewed its snow-covered surface.

The traces of their footsteps were clearly visible. A farmer from his house near by saw them and gave the alarm. The parachutists lay watching the preparations for their capture. They had very little ammunition, but were ready to fight, though their position, surrounded as they were on all sides, was hopeless. Presently three pointers appeared leading a motley collection of village dogs, followed by village children. These in turn were being briskly pursued by their mothers, who cried out to them to come back immediately, and behind the mothers were the fathers issuing similar orders to their wives. Last of all, and some distance behind, came regular troops and a number of carabinieri. To open fire would have placed the women and children in grave peril ; "Pritchard had no choice but to surrender."

In the meanwhile Daly and his five men, who had been dropped in the wrong valley, were also trying to escape. Soon after landing they had heard the sound of explosions and realized that the task had been accomplished and that nothing, therefore, remained for them to do but to make their way as speedily as possible to the rendezvous. Dawn on February 15th found them eighteen miles from it, short of food, and very short of sleep. Since they had to reach the mouth of the Sele that night it was necessary to move by day. About 11 a.m. they fell in with a number of soldiers, police and civilians, to whom they explained that they were German airmen on special duty who had to reach Naples by two o'clock that afternoon. A car must be immediately provided. Bystanders appealed to the local mayor, but, becoming suspicious, he demanded papers from Daly, and since none were forthcoming, handcuffed the parachutists and chained them together. In this condition they arrived at Naples, where they were threatened with death.

In the end, all save one were put in a prison camp, the exception being the interpreter, Picchi. He was severely questioned, court-martialled, and then shot.

Had this gallant band of parachutists been able to reach the mouth of the Sele disappointment, not a submarine, would have awaited them. The orders of H.M.S. "Triumph" had been countermanded as the result of an unhappy and wholly unpredictable coincidence. It will be remembered that the two Whitleys loaded with bombs had been dispatched to create a diversion. One of them, carrying Norman, successfully accomplished its task and dropped bombs on the railway yard at Foggia, causing explosions and fires. Passing Sicily on its way back, it dropped its last bomb on a railway.

The other Whitley, however, was not so fortunate. Engine trouble developed, and the pilot sent out a signal in cipher saying that he was about to make a forced landing near the mouth of the river Sele. He chose this spot because the Whitley happened to be near it at the time, not because he knew that a British submarine might be in the offing. This fact had been kept a closely guarded secret and communicated only to the Officers commanding the parachute troops. It was at once realized that this signal sent by the Whitley would be picked up by the enemy, and, since the code in which it had been transmitted was not of a very elaborate kind, would soon be deciphered the Italian garrisons and police in the neighbourhood would be warned, and thus the submarine lying off a few hundred yards from shore would in all probability be detected. This placed the High Command in a terrible predicament. Submarines and their highly trained crews are very valuable, but, even so, the risk would have been accepted and an attempt made to rescue the parachute troops had there seemed to be the slightest possibility of success. Prolonged consideration, however, showed that the chances were negligible, and the decision was taken that a submarine should not be sent. The operation had a negligible effect on the war in Albania or North Africa, nor was the water supply of Apulia interrupted for any great length of time. The aqueduct was repaired before the local reservoirs in the towns served ran dry. On the other hand the alarm and consternation caused throughout Italy was considerable. The area was barred to neutrals, far more stringent air raid precautions were imposed, and a large number of guards posted. These precautions, all quite unnecessary, endured until Italy surrendered more than two years later.

A raid to learn a secret

Just over a year elapsed before British parachute troops were again in action. It was the enemy who staged the next action in which airborne troops took part. On May 20th, 1941, they invaded Crete in force with parachutists and glider-borne troops. Eleven days' fierce fighting gained them possession of the island, and the world learnt for the first time what a mass assault by an army of this kind could accomplish. True, the cost was very high, The German parachute battalions and glider-borne brigades if suffered enormous casualties. Had it been possible, which it was not, for reasons not germane to this account, for the British garrison in Crete to have been provided with air support, there is little doubt that the airborne invasion would have failed. Be that as it may, the profit was not entirely "on the enemy's side of the ledger. Many lessons of the highest importance were learnt by those in command, eager by study and argument to discover from what had happened above the airfields and olive-yards of Crete the best way, both strategic and tactical, to use airborne forces.

It was at this time that a few Hotspur gliders made their appearance, and night glider flying began, the gliders being towed by Hectors. The Horsa glider was making its first trial flights, and the Hamilcar had emerged from the stage of design. But there were not available in any quantity men or equipment, aircraft or gliders, and the airborne division which Browning was appointed to command in November of that year existed mostly on paper. Its development followed closely the Prime Minister's dictum concerning the production of munitions of war: "In the first year nothing at all; second year very little; third year quite a lot; fourth year all you want." Nevertheless, within four months of his appointment Browning was able to stage an operation small, it is true, but one most perfectly planned and executed, an operation, indeed, which bade fair to become a model of its kind.

Along the coast of western Europe the Germans had established a chain of radiolocation posts designed to give warning of the approach of hostile aircraft or ships. That they had done so had long been known to the British Intelligence Services, and many photographs had been taken of these installations. Their precise nature, however, was still a matter for argument and conjecture among experts. Photographs, however skilfully taken-and in that art the Photographic Reconnaissance Units of the Royal Air Force have no equal-could not betray all the secrets it was desired to discover, for many of them were hidden behind thick walls. The capture of one of these apparatus and its examination by scientists might possibly enable British installations to be improved, though that was doubtful, for British development in this field has always been ahead of German ; but it would certainly enable scientists to discover how far the enemy had made progress, how accurate the process of detection had become, and, therefore, what risks British bombers flying to the attack might have to meet because of its presence, A sudden swoop upon an installation and its removal, if possible intact, would be of singular value to the pilots and crews of Bomber Command.

Could such a swoop be made ? The planning staff of Combined Operations, then under the direction of Acting Vice-Admiral the Lord Louis Mountbatten, G.C.V.O., D.S.O., A.D.C., thought that it could. The First Airborne Division and 38 Wing of the R.A.F. were called into consultation, and in the beginning of 1942 the design began to grow. It did not take long to discover the whereabouts of an apparatus of the kind desired by the scientists. There was one which fulfilled all their requirements situated close to the small village of Bruneval, some twelve miles north-north-east of Le Havre. It had been erected in front of an isolated house standing in wide fields with high cliffs beyond rising above the sea. Some 400 yards away was a garrisoned farmhouse called Le Presbytere, encircled by a wood.

Within a short distance the cliffs sloped down to a small beach or cove whence a rough road led to the village of Bruneval a short distance inland.

If the radiolocation post could be captured and held for sufficient time to enable the apparatus to be dismantled, it could be removed, brought to the cove, and then, together with its captors, taken back to England by the Royal Navy.

A closer study of the position showed that it was defended by fifteen posts manned by a garrison numbering about a hundred, while farther inland a regiment of infantry and an armoured battalion could serve as immediate reinforcements.

Trained parachutists, it was decided, should carry out the operation. As with the attack on the aqueduct in southern Italy, immediate rehearsals were put in hand, in which the crews of the Whitleys who were to convey the force to Bruneval took part. The aircraft were led by Wing Commander Pickard, D.S.O. and bar, D.F.C., destined two years later to die for his country and-" for France leading an even more hazardous and equally successful attack.

On the night of February 27th/28th conditions were perfect, "no wind . . . and a bright moon with a little cloud and a very light haze." In the half-darkness six officers and 113 other ranks, among them nine sappers and four signallers, entered the waiting Whitleys. With them was Flight Sergeant E. W. F. Cox, an expert radio engineer. It was he who had volunteered to dismantle the radiolocation apparatus, and he had learnt how to use a parachute in the short space of three weeks. The force was commanded by Major J. D. Frost, whose men, like himself, were in high spirits. Wrapped in warm sleeping bags they whiled away the flight with cards and songs "Annie Laurie," "Lulu " and "Come sit by my side if you love me" the special song of the parachute troops, being the favourites. Flight Sergeant Cox obliged with a solo rendering of "The Rose of Tralee." The flight was uneventful and the navigation perfect, except in the case of two Whitleys, one carrying Lieutenant E. C. B. Charteris, which were compelled by flak to take avoiding action and thus arrived late and not quite in the right place.

It was a model attack

The plan was for Frost to attack the isolated house near the apparatus and kill or capture its crew, who probably lived there. A second party which included Flight Sergeant Cox and the sappers, were to go straight to the post itself and dismantle it, while a third, under Charteris was to secure the beach near by from which the parachutists would be taken off by the Navy.

Timing was of great importance. The force must remain ashore be carried off themselves before enemy reinforcements could arrive or the movements of the tide prevent the Navy from coming in to the beach All went Well with Frost and his party, and with those detailed to seize the apparatus. Such Germans as there were, either in the house or in the defences close by, were killed or captured in the first rush and Cox with the aid of Lieutenant Vernon and his engineers successfully removed the apparatus from the hole in the ground from which it protruded. This took some little time, and towards the end they were under fire, two bullets striking a part of the machinery as Cox held it in his hands Frost., Vernon and the engineers then began to move towards the beach When they reached it, they discovered that it had not yet been captured What had happened was this. Charteris and his men, as has been explained had been dropped somewhat late and in the Wrong valley. It looked very like the right one," records Charteris, "but there was no row of trees at the bottom of it as there should have been, and it was not deep enough. I don't mind saying that that was a nasty moment." Their landing had been for just so long as it would take to seize and remove their objective, and then perfect for there was no wind, and when Charteris touched the ground the "rigging lines of his parachute fell softly round him" ; but he did not know where he was. Looking up, he heard and then saw aircraft passing overhead flying a steady course and judged that they were the other Whitleys and that they had not yet dropped their parachutists. Since they were flying north, he thought it best to move in that direction too. He did so with his men, at a rapid lope which is the gait of the parachutist, being something between a fast walk and a trot. Presently he caught sight of the lighthouse at Cap d'Antifer, and then he knew where he was. Almost immediately the party ran into some Germans. One of them accompanied the parachutists for some distance, they taking him for one of themselves, he under the impression they belonged to a German patrol. Subsequent explanations resulted in the death of the German.

The party then crossed the ravine near Bruneval village and came under life. Hearing sounds of battle ahead, they rightly concluded that the radiolocation post was being attacked, and made towards it. Presently Charteris fell in with his commanding officer, explained the situation, and was ordered to rush the cove.

He and his men moved off downhill. "I felt as naked as a baby because I was only about seventy yards from the house on the beach, which I knew to be held by the enemy. We . . . flung two volleys of hand grenades into the balcony of the house." They then charged, and captured it while others killed the garrison of a nearby pill-box. In the house a solitary German telephone orderly surrendered with the instrument in his hand. He explained that at that moment he had been talking with his commanding officer, who had complained bitterly of the noise the orderly was making at his end of the telephone. His explanation that the din was caused by the grenades of the enemy was cut short when the parachutists burst into the room.

Having captured the beach, the raiders sat down to await the coming of the Navy, Frost signalling from time to time in the direction of the sea with a blue-shaded torch. Soon after half-past two in the morning, assault landing craft covered by support craft were seen coming in the moonlight.

First the apparatus, which they had fought so successfully to capture, then the prisoners, then the wounded, and finally the rest of the force, all but seven who had become separated and were left behind, were embarked and reached England unmolested, under cover provided, when day dawned, by Spitfires of Fighter Command. The success of this small operation was complete. At a cost of one killed, seven wounded, and seven missing, a valuable piece of apparatus had been brought safely to England.

The next day a Hurricane flying over Bruneval and Le

Presbytere saw a number of German officers standing in conference round the hole which had been the home of the apparatus and which now gaped wide and empty.

The pilot dived and opened fire with his machine-guns. The hole was quickly occupied.

The first British glider operation In the next two raids, the first on St. Nazaire in March, the second on Dieppe in August, airborne troops took no part. The original plans for the Dieppe raid provided for the destruction by parachutists of the two coastal batteries to the east and west of the town ; but the change of date from June to August necessitated a change of plan, and Commando troops took the place of airborne.

A third small raid may here be conveniently described. On November 19th, 1942, two Halifaxes, towing two Horsa gliders, set off from an airfield in Scotland for an objective in southern Norway. The importance of the objective was such that all risks had to be taken. [The objective was a heavy-water plant connected with German research on the atomic bomb. A later raid on this plant was successful.] This was the first time that British gliders set out to attack the enemy. They were flown, one by Sergeant M. F. C. Strathdee and Sergeant P. Doig of the Glider Pilot Regiment, the other by Pilot Officer Davis and Sergeant Fraser of the Royal Australian Air Force. Each glider carried fifteen sappers, all volunteers, under the command of Lieutenant Methven, G.M. Their task was to destroy the objective, and the difficulties were great. In the first place, the towing of gliders was an art in which the crews had not as yet had much practice. Secondly, the tugs had to be adapted and their engines, having to pull the added weight of the glider behind, developed defects, particularly in the cooling system. Fortunately these and other troubles were discovered during the practice tows and were remedied, so that on the night of the operation two Halifaxes were serviceable, though a third held in reserve could not be flown. The greatest difficulty of all was that caused by the distance to be covered, some 400 miles, and the necessity for extremely accurate navigation over the mountainous district in which the objective lay.

In every air operation all ultimately depends on the weather, and on this occasion a correct forecast was of vital importance. On the morning of the attempt, thick cloud for most of the way, but clear skies and a good moon over the target area were promised. The two Halifaxes took off while it was still light and set course for Norway. Almost immediately the inter-communication system connecting the gliders and the tugs broke down. One Halifax kept low, seeking to fly beneath the cloud and then to gain height on nearing the Norwegian coast, where the pilot hoped for clear weather. What happened is not exactly known, but at some moment the tug hit the side of a mountain, crashed, and all its crew were killed. The violence of the shock loosed the glider, which made a very heavy landing close by, killing and injuring several of its occupants.

The other Halifax was more fortunate. It flew high and approached the Norwegian coast at 10,000 feet. Here, as promised, the weather cleared, but it was found impossible to locate the landing zone. Though they were the best that could be got, the maps were exceedingly inaccurate, and the necessary pin-point could not therefore be obtained. The whole district was covered with snow which made the identification of objects on the ground even more difficult. The pilot of the Halifax, Squadron Leader A, B. Wilkinson, with his commanding officer, Group Captain T. B. Cooper, D.F.C., on board, made every effort to find the right spot, until, with petrol running low, he was forced to turn for home. The glider was still at the end of the rope, but on crossing the coast the combination ran into heavy cloud and icing conditions, the air became very bumpy, and the two parted. This glider, too, made land and crashed not very far from the other. The survivors of both gliders were captured and almost immediately fell into the hands of the Gestapo.

CHAPTER 5

THE RED DEVILS OF NORTH AFRICA

ON NOVEMBER 8th, 1942, great operations of war, for which many preparations had been made both in England and America, were launched. That day saw the landing of the Allies at several points on the coasts of French North Africa. The troops went ashore from fleets of transports protected by warships and squadrons of aircraft, all three Services thus taking part in a combined operation of which the grandeur was surpassed only by the expedition which invaded Normandy nineteen months later. Not all the troops who had a share in this "majestic enterprise" were carried in ships.

Some arrived on the field of battle by parachute, transported thither by troop-carrying aircraft. The troops were British and belonged to the 1st Airborne Division ; the aircraft were American and came from three Groups of the 51st Transport Wing of the United States Army Air Force. It is the exploits of these men which must now be recounted.

The object of General Eisenhower, Supreme Commander, was to occupy all that part of North Africa which owed allegiance to Marshal Pétain and the Vichy regime. Though the Allied strength deployed was considerable, for the invading forces were large and might therefore reasonably be relied upon to overcome any opposition, it was hoped and believed that they would be welcomed by at least the great majority of those who dwelt in this vast land of fertile coastal plain and rugged, inhospitable mountain.

Nor were these hopes falsified. Resistance there was in some places, notably at Oran, where several units of the French Navy fought with a forlorn gallantry worthy of a better cause ; but by the evening of November 10th that port was in our hands, American troops were in Casablanca and British and American in Algiers.

Though taken entirely by surprise, the counter of the Germans was swift.

By November 11th, Unoccupied France had been entered and Italian troops were in Nice. It was obvious that, once he had recovered from the first shock, the enemy would react with the greatest vigour. Rommel's army, defeated at El Alamein at the beginning of the month, was streaming westward, and at the time of General Eisenhower's landing was fighting rearguard actions in Sollum and Sidi Barrani, having in fifteen days lost 40,000 prisoners and the Commander of the Afrika Korps. Rommel was now faced by a threat to his rear, the size of which he could not at that time gauge but which was obviously of the most formidable kind. Would the German High Command leave him to his fate, or would they seek to continue the 'fight and, if unable to drive back the invaders in the west, at least make certain that what remained of their forces in Africa should still find a way of escape to Sicily and thence to the Italian mainland ? The key to the situation was the great port of Tunis. If that fell into the hands of the Allies, the armies of Von Arnim and Rommel were doomed.

More than 500 miles of difficult country separates Algiers from Tunis, where Von Armin was seeking to establish himself in considerable force.

The British 1st Army under General Anderson set out to forestall and, if they arrived too late, to do battle with him. Rather more than half-way between Algiers and Tunis lies the port of Bone, which possesses a good airfield. To take it was an immediate and obvious object. Plans to do so had been maturing for some time. On November 12th they were put into execution.

The race to capture Bone airfield

On that day a task force consisting of two company groups and a head-quarters group, comprising some 360 officers and men belonging to the 3rd Battalion of the 1st Parachute Brigade, under the command of Lieutenant-Colonel R. J. Pine-Coffin, arrived over the airfield in the early morning. They were carried in C.47 aircraft (Dakotas) of No. 60 Group of the United States Army Air Force. The long journey of the Brigade had begun in England late on the 9th, and they had flown through the night to reach Gibraltar in the morning. Here they rested for half a day, checking their equipment and making final preparations. They were off again in the darkness that precedes dawn and arrived some hours later at the airfield of Maison Blanche, close to Algiers. Here once more they waited, faced by the final stage of their journey. Leaving the ground at first light on the 12th, they reached Bone at about 8.30 in the morning. By then their numbers had been reduced from 450 to 360. Two aircraft had developed defects and been unable to leave England, and two more had fallen by the way, one having crashed in flames between Gibraltar and Algiers. The occupants of the other, which came down in the sea between Gibraltar and Algiers, were picked up by an American ship on her way to New York, all save Captain Crichton, who was drowned rescuing one of his men. The parachutists rejoined their regiment two months later, travelling to North Africa by way of the U.S.A. and the United Kingdom.

The detachment of the 3rd Battalion were well aware of what was expected of them. They were engaged in a race against time. A German parachute battalion was known, or thought to be at Tunis and might at any moment take off with the object of seizing their objective before they reached it.

"This," said Captain James Moore, adjutant of the battalion, "added to the excitement."

The drop was made in a scattered pattern covering some three miles of stony ground. Some containers fell a mile short. Stony it was indeed.

Moreover, the air in Africa is thinner than English air and the parachutists 'were heavily laden. Each man was carrying a considerable quantity of small-arms ammunition, and this was over and above what was in the containers.

The drop was made from a height of about 400 feet. In accomplishing it one officer was particularly unfortunate. He fell so heavily that he was unconscious for four days. His comrades carried him to a nearby house where headquarters was established, and placed him on a fine bed with brass knobs at its four corners. From time to time he was heard to murmur: "I'll have a little more of the turbot, waiter." There was only one fatal casualty, one man accidentally shooting himself with his Sten gun during the drop, but thirteen men were injured.

The operation was successful, for the airfield was captured. The presence of parachute troops helped considerably to raise the hearts of the local French inhabitants and the expectations of the Arabs. These paid particular attention to the parachute containers and their contents, and a quantity of arms and ammunition disappeared with startling suddenness. Moreover, the task of persuading them to hand over what they regarded, not unnaturally perhaps, as a silken gift from Heaven was not easy, especially when one of them pointed out that not less than 544 sets of silk underclothing could be made from one parachute and sold at great profit.

Together with No. 6 Commando the task force held the airfield under constant attack from Focke-Wulfs and Messerschmitts for a week; till they were withdrawn and joined the remainder of their battalion. They had accomplished their task, thanks to the co-operation of our American Allies, who provided all the aircraft necessary to transport them and their comrades in the other battalions. This they did despite the fact

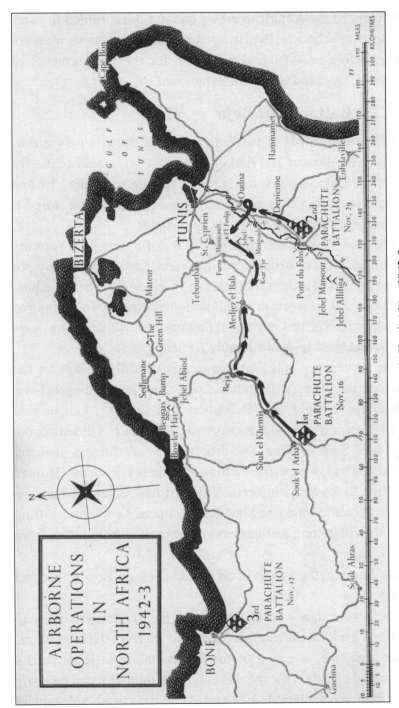

Airborne operations in North Africa 1942-3

that many of the American crews had not been trained to carry and drop parachutists. British aircraft and trained crews were not yet available in sufficient numbers, for the requirements of Bomber Command were still paramount.

The 1st Battalion at Beja

While two-thirds of the 3rd Parachute Battalion were thus engaged, the 1st and 2nd Battalions and the remainder of the 3rd had arrived successfully at Algiers by sea. Between the 13th and 15th of November they collected their equipment and stored it in readiness at the Maison Blanche airfield.

The task, especially that of the R.A.F. parachute packing section attached to Brigade Headquarters, had not been easy, for there was a total lack of transport and stevedores. The parachute packers went to work in a requisitioned cinema and laboured without pause or rest night and day until every parachute, over 3,000, had been re-packed ready for instant use.

On November 16th, after an unsuccessful attempt on the previous day, the 1st Battalion under its commanding officer, Lieutenant-Colonel (now Brigadier) Hill, D.S.O., M.C., carried by 64 Group of the American Army Air Force, landed on the plain near Souk el Arba. The drop was successful, but one man was killed and two others, victims of what is known as " Roman candling," severely injured. This mishap occurs when the parachute leaves the pack but fails to open, its wearer hurtling to earth with a long and useless streamer of silk fluttering from his shoulders.

On landing, the battalion advanced through Beja to Medjez el Bah.

They were thus well in advance of the 1st Army seeking to establish itself on the plain dividing the sea from the mountains. Their presence, like that of the 3rd Battalion at Bone, had a heartening effect on the local French, and their feat can be justly described as remarkable. Throughout this and subsequent operations the help they and the rest of the Division received from French forces operating in advance and to the flank of the 1st Army was considerable. No reconnaissance had been made, and their objective was changed a few hours before the take-off from Souk el Arba to Beja, about forty-five miles from the place where they dropped. On landing Lieutenant-Colonel Hill immediately marched his battalion twice through the town, the men wearing on the first occasion their steel helmets and on the second their red berets. So impressed was he by their bearing and what he thought was their numbers that the French commander and his men joined the battalion and fought by their side. Here they captured a number of armoured cars and reconnaissance vehicles, and here the Colonel was badly wounded. He and his adjutant, Captain Whitelock, with their two orderlies, attacked two German tanks, disposed of the first with gammon bombs and were about to receive the surrender of the second tank's commander, who had raised his hands, when his machine-gunner opened fire, badly wounding both officers. The crews of all the German tanks were thereupon wiped out.

For his conduct in this battle, and for other gallant actions, Lieutenant-Colonel Hill received the Distinguished Service Order. His place as commanding officer of the battalion was taken by Major (now Lieutenant-Colonel) A. S. Pearson, D.S.O., M.C., who within less than a fortnight had won the Distinguished Service Order and the Military Cross. The official reports of those days of confused and heavy fighting describe his conduct as one of " superb gallantry." He was ably seconded by the men he led so well. In one action those in charge of the three-inch mortars carried them nine miles, fought them, took part in a bayonet charge, and returned to their starting point within a period of eleven hours. The 1st Battalion was presently joined by the 3rd Battalion, and on December 6th part of the Parachute Brigade found itself fighting as ordinary infantry under its commander, Brigadier E. W. C. Flavell, D.S.O., M.C.

They formed part of the Fifth Corps, and attached to them were No. 1 Commando, two French battalions and an American artillery unit.

The 2nd Battalion strikes at Oudna

Before giving an account of the heavy lighting in which they took part during the next four months, the adventures of the 2nd Battalion must be related in some detail, for they were indeed remarkable. Kept at first in reserve at the Maison Blanche, it was decided to use them to attack two enemy airfields, one at Pont du Fahs and the other at Depienne, both almost due south of Tunis and well beyond the area of Souk el Arba where the remainder of the brigade was established. Having destroyed the German aircraft and stores on these airfields, the 2nd Battalion was to move to Oudna, still nearer to Tunis, repeat its performance and then strike north-west to join up with the leading elements of the British 1st Army in the neighbourhood of St. Cyprien.

On November 29th, shortly before they were due to take off, information came to hand that the airfields at Pont du Fahs and Depienne had been abandoned by the Germans. It was decided, therefore, that the battalion should land near the third objective, Oudna. The force, carried by aircraft of No. 60 and No. 64 American Group, under the protection of long-range Hurricanes, Lightnings and Spitfires, was on the way to its objectives by 12.30 p.m. Bad weather had made previous reconnaissance impossible, and it was left to the battalion commander, Lieutenant-Colonel J, D. Frost, D.S.O., M.C., who had led the highly successful raid on Bruneval and was travelling in the leading aircraft, to share with the pilot the responsibility of choosing the dropping zone from the air. The force Hew high to clear the mountains ; it became very cold ; the air was bumpy, and some of the men suffered from air-sickness. About thirty miles from Depienne they began to descend until the battalion was flying at 600 feet. The dropping zone chosen was mostly ploughland with a watercourse dividing it.

At ten minutes to three in the afternoon, the first stick dropped, followed quickly by the remainder, and the battalion came down over an area one-and-a-half miles long and half a mile broad. One man was killed in the drop. "A" and "C" Companies held the boundaries of the dropping zone, while "B" Company was ordered to occupy Depienne and lay hands on all available transport. A number of men injured in the drop were put into the schoolhouse, where they were well treated by the local French inhabitants.

That evening the battalion formed up to begin its advance on Oudna. It moved off soon after 1 a.m., carrying some of its mortars and ammunition in mule carts. Many mortars, however, had to be borne on the backs of those who were to take them into action, and their weight became an increasing cause of fatigue. The way was mostly over steep, rough tracks crossing stony hills, and the battalion moved through the bitter night to the inhospitable accompaniment of barking dogs. At 4.30 in the morning of November 30th, after covering twelve miles, they lay down to rest, but, being without blankets, found the cold too keen for sleep. At first light they moved off again, with "B" Company acting as advance guard, till by mid-morning they had reached a well called the Prise de L'eau. Here all available mules, donkeys and horses were commandeered from the local Arabs, who informed the commanding officer that the landing ground at Oudna was not occupied, and that the Axis troops were withdrawing to Tunis. By now, great cold had given place to uncomfortable heat, but the objective was in sight, wide and deserted except for one crashed German -aircraft in its midst.

The advance began in the afternoon, "A" Company was in the van, "B" Company to the right marching along a dominating ridge, and "C" Company to the left, with battalion headquarters and the mortars. An hour later "A" Company was in action and, very skilfully handled by its commander, Major Ashford, had driven the enemy to the north of the landing field, while the rest of the battalion occupied Oudna railway station close by. By four in the afternoon the landing ground was reached and, as was suspected, found to be deserted. Four native tents, thought to contain stores, turned out to be hayricks.

"Dropped from the blue in to the blue"

By then, however, the Germans were beginning to take the measure of the situation. At 4.30 five of their heavy tanks appeared west of the landing ground and began to shell "C" Company, killing one of its officers.

Some of the men, moving from one piece of cover to the next- it was mostly rocks and bushes- got close enough to the nearest tank to throw gammon bombs at it. Whether or not it was damaged, however, was uncertain.

The German tank commander was cautious and made no attempt to move against the parachutists, but lay off and kept the airfield under machine-gun fire. He was presently joined by a number of Messerschmitts which carried out very low-flying machine-gun attacks. Though they caused no casualties, they made all movement impossible. Since ammunition was precious, the orders were that no aircraft was to be tired at. The men relied on their camouflage smocks and netting to protect them from observation, and in this they were not disappointed.

"Now as the whole object of the mission," says Frost in his report, "had been to destroy aircraft on Oudna, and as there were no aircraft to destroy, I made plans for moving westwards to link up with the First Army."

The position of the Parachute Battalion should be realized. They had, as it were, been dropped from the blue into the blue, many miles ahead of the ground army and its patrols. There was nothing but their own resources on which to live, march and fight, save for such transport, mostly mules, on which they had been, or might be, able to lay hands. Their defensive positions on and round the landing ground at Oudna were very insecure ; the enemy had had several hours in which to make a full reconnaissance and, therefore, to gauge the numbers against him, and his armoured forces were already moving up in considerable strength.

At dusk, "C" Company, which had been on the left, moved back with orders to enter the hills behind "B" Company. They were soon engaged with the enemy by the light of, the flaming hayricks, which had at first been mistaken for storage huts. The sound of explosions indicated that the enemy was possibly destroying an ammunition dump, and the commanding officer debated whether to launch an attack. By then, however, the condition of "A" and "C" Companies was such that it became imperative to reorganise and rest. At nine in the evening the battalion moved off back to the positions which it had quitted that morning round Prise de L'eau. It reached them one-and-a-half hours later, and the men were at last able to rest, if rest it could be called, for the night was again bitterly cold and sleep almost out of the question.

The next morning Frost received news by wireless which might have caused a man less stout of heart to quail. The British armoured thrust against Tunis had been postponed, and the one chance, never very strong, that he and his men would be able to join forces that day with the advancing tanks, had therefore disappeared. He was almost, if not quite, surrounded. The enemy had large numbers of lorry-borne infantry near at hand, and every road was patrolled by their armoured cars. The battalion was only fifteen miles from Tunis itself, and some thirty to forty miles from Medjez el Bab and Tebourba, the nearest places at which other British troops might possibly be encountered.

Ambush in a bottle-neck

There were two small consolations. The three companies

were so disposed as to make an all-round defence possible, and there was water. Frost was confident that he would be able to repel anything less than a full-scale attack. He decided to remain where he was until noon, then to move back into the hills, wait there till nightfall, and only venture on to the plains in darkness. At one point the approaches to his position ran through what he describes as a bottle-neck between two ridges. Here he arranged an ambush, giving orders that no enemy vehicles, moving up the road to engage them, were to be fired upon until they were well inside the bottle-neck. About ten in the morning two enemy tanks, two armoured cars, and two lorries towing guns approached from the north and halted three-quarters of a mile away. One of the armoured cars went forward alone and surprised a small party of parachutists filling their water bottles at the well from which the place took its name. The commander of the car, an Italian officer, who was leaning from the turret, was shot, but the gammon bomb thrown at his vehicle missed and it made off. No further movement was made, the enemy contenting himself with shelling the parachutists, who replied vigorously with mortar bombs, inflicted casualties and compelled a withdrawal.

The attack from the north had been a failure. The next was put in from the south and would have to pass through the bottle-neck. It opened an hour later, when two armoured cars and a tank were seen moving along the road. Covering the position was a section of men under an N.C.O. armed with an anti-tank rifle. As the leading armoured car drew near he saw displayed upon it two yellow triangles, which was the recognition device of the First Army. Relief appeared to be at hand, and the N.C.O., leaving the post, went forward displaying his own triangle, only to fall a victim to this ruse de guerre. He was seized, taken prisoner, and made to walk in front of the armoured car till it reached his section and captured them.

He was then sent to Frost with a message from the enemy

demanding surrender since the battalion was surrounded. The demand was refused and an attempt made to attack the German vehicles, which could not be tired upon for they were sheltering in a deep depression. Presently they made off, and the battalion settled down to endure some desultory shelling.

But not for long. At noon Frost began his move into the hills, "A" Company acting as rearguard. The wounded were placed in a nearby farm, and Lieutenant MacGavin, R.A.M.C., left in charge of them. By half-past two in the afternoon the parachutists had reached the hills at a place where there was a spring and where good observation could be had. Here they lay for half an hour, and were then attacked on all sides, the brunt of the assault being borne by "C" Company, who beat off all infantry attacks at a cost to itself of heavy casualties caused by mortar fire coming from behind some farm-houses.

During this attack two tanks were knocked out by gammon bombs and two others immobilised. Their fate was accomplished very largely by Private Wilkinson, who crawled out of cover and attacked them with an anti-tank rifle; moving from boulder to boulder, he kept this weapon in action till they were all knocked out or subdued. But he did so only at the cost of his life. At five in the afternoon the enemy tried an air attack.

Messerschmitt 109s flew low over the position, but opened fire not on Frost and his men but on their own troops, mistaking them for the parachutists, who were almost invisible. During the weary months of training in England they had learnt the art and the necessity of taking cover, and they had been most attentive pupils.

The hard road through the hills Night was now at hand and the attack, everywhere held, fell away. Even the shelling ceased. Frost decided to withdraw by groups of individual companies, giving the village of Massicault as the rendezvous. "B" Company was to lead, and would then be followed by Battalion Headquarters and the mortar platoon. "A" Company and the remnants of "C" brought up the rear. By then the casualties in the battalion were about 150 killed and wounded. As soon as it was quite dark, Frost set his hunting horn to his lips and blew the signal to begin the retreat. The road down to the plain was very steep and difficult in the dark, and when at length the level ground was reached, the stumbling, weary men encountered wide stretches of ploughland where the going was very heavy. By then "all ranks were feeling exhausted. We had had no real rest for forty-eight hours and had been moving over mountainous country all that time. Also very heavy loads had been carried." Some men's feet had been badly cut, and since there had been no time to give them proper medical attention, the wounds were now festering. During that night two deep river beds had to be crossed, as well as the river Miliane, which provided water for the water-bottles but "it was brackish and only just drinkable." At one o'clock in the morning they rested for an hour and a half, and it was then discovered that Major Teichman, the second in command, and Captain Short, the adjutant, were missing.

The march was resumed, and by six o'clock the battalion was a mile north-east of the Djebel el Mengoub, high ground not far from the village of Massicault which was their destination. It was decided to halt until daylight. As soon as the sun began to appear, Lieutenant Charteris took a small reconnoitring party towards a farm-house. He was back half an hour later with the welcome news that there were good shelter, plenty of water, and friendly Arabs at the farm, and that they had told him that Massicault was still in the hands of the enemy. Battalion Headquarters moved in immediately. A guard was mounted and "the men cooked breakfast and washed."

Soon after ten o'clock Major Ashford arrived to say that "A" Company, numbering about a hundred men, were safely round a farm half a mile to the east. Its inhabitants, who were French, had warned him that German armoured cars frequently patrolled the area. At the same time Frost learnt that the nearest Allied forces were said to be at Furna, not far from Massicault. Once more he decided to hold on, fight until dusk, and then seek to withdraw. Lieutenant Charteris, who had won the Military Cross at Bruneval, and two men were sent to Furna with orders to get into contact with the Allied Forces if they were there, and to return at all costs before dark.

At noon "A" Company arrived and Frost then established his lines of defence around the farm, which was called El Fedja. It seemed to him that the enemy would be unable to mount any considerable attack until fairly late in the day. If only, therefore, his exhausted but indomitable men could hold out till sunset, there was a chance of escape. Everyone was ordered to lie quiet at his post and not to move. About one o'clock a column of enemy armoured cars was seen approaching slowly, and an hour later his infantry was observed setting up mortars and machine-gun posts on a ridge to the north of El Fedja. Not a man of the battalion stirred, and "this silence on our part seemed to mystify the enemy." In the middle of the afternoon he opened the first phase of his attack, by directing heavy but ineffective mortar and machine-gun fire on the orchard next to the farm.

Towards dusk the machine-gun fire increased in intensity, but the bullets went high, and it seemed to the parachutists, still holding on in grim silence, that the enemy were tiring at each other, or perhaps even that some units of the First Army had arrived to the south and were being engaged by the enemy. "Some of the more imaginative men fancied they heard words being shouted in English .... Towards dusk the enemy became very bold, and a party of two officers approached to within five yards of the cactus hedge surrounding the orchard. They were killed with grenades and Sten gun tire."

The last rally - the last chance

By then Frost had issued his orders for the night's retreat. When the sound of his horn was heard every man was to leave his position, run past Battalion Headquarters, and on to the south-east towards the high ground at Jebel el Mengoub, where the battalion would rally. This was their last, their only, chance. "We had not sufficient ammunition left to tight another battle, and I estimated that the enemy were approximately four to one stronger in number." Lieutenant Charteris, who it will be remembered had been sent earlier in the day to get into touch with Allied forces said to be at Furna, had not yet returned. He was never seen again.

At six in the evening the Germans launched their main attack and it was repelled with considerable loss, one section of it being wiped out with Sten-gun tire and the last of the grenades. A quarter of an hour later Frost sounded his horn and the men moved off according to plan. The enemy made no further attack, but in the darkness the parachutists, now almost at their last gasp, found it very difficult to keep in touch with one another.

Towards morning they reached another farm-house owned by a Frenchman who warned Frost that an Arab, known to be in the pay of the Germans, had made off to inform the enemy of their whereabouts. The battalion quitted the friendly shelter of the farm for the barren heights near Ksar Tyr.

From their summit a glad sight met the eyes of these weary men. In the middle distance was Medjez el Bab and the main road dividing the tumbled plain, and at that moment an Arab, running up, told Frost that the town was strongly held by the Allies.

A number of orchards lay between them and the main road, and through these they moved in open formation, taking advantage of the cover they afforded. In the last they halted, ate a meal, and soon after one o'clock in the afternoon reached the road. Along it they marched, and soon an armoured vehicle was seen bumping and rolling across country. It reached the road at a point ahead of them, turned and made towards them. It was an American reconnaissance car. Contact with the First Army had at last been made.

So ended a lighting retreat conducted by men most of whom had not seen action before, and costing sixteen officers and 250 other ranks.

After another eight days of marching, counter-marching and fighting, the battalion was relieved by the Coldstream Guards and taken by lorry to Souk el Khemis, where at last they were able to rest. Their spirit is best shown by two stories of what happened to some of them who were captured by the enemy during that arduous retreat. A corporal, who was a medical student in time of peace, was wounded and captured. He had been hit in the arm, which was placed in a sling, but he contrived to hide in it his fighting knife. After dark he watched his opportunity, stabbed the German guard in the back, freed his companions, and they all reached the British lines in safety. "A number of men of the battalion were captured and were being taken to bondage in an Italian lorry escorted by Italian armoured cars.

One of them overpowered one of the escort, seized his pistol, shot the driver of the lorry, and escaped with his companions across country, eluding the pursuit of the armoured cars. They, too, reached safety. Such men as these are truly formidable, and such feats soon caused the parachute troops to be known as "the Red Devils," a name bestowed upon them by the enemy in March 1943. It was derived from the colour of their berets.

We must now return to the rest of the Parachute Brigade.

After the capture of the Bone airfield by part of the 3rd Battalion, this formation moved into the mountainous area north of Beja and became involved in desultory fighting which went on throughout the greater part of December. It was during this period that Lieutenant Livesey of the 1st Parachute Squadron of the Royal Engineers, together with a sergeant and two sappers, carried out a thirty-six-hour reconnaissance behind the enemy lines and brought back a comprehensive report on the state of the tracks and roads in an area which it was proposed to attack. At one moment the sergeant was compelled to remain motionless for more than two hours, his head resting on his hand and his elbow on a bed of sharp stones. Throughout that time a German sentry was but five yards away and the slightest movement would have meant the discovery of the others. The sergeant's arm remained numb and useless for the rest of the patrol.

The Airborne fight as infantry

The weather in the North African hills during that month resembled the climate of the western highlands of Scotland in September. The rainfall was heavy, but it was broken by periods of delightful sunshine. Frost and snow in the upper levels prevailed at night, and the general conditions under foot were wet and muddy. The troops lived as hard as they fought ; amenities were few and luxuries non-existent, but oranges and vegetables were cheap and plentiful. Relations with the local inhabitants, a mixture of "French colonists, half-breeds of various shades and colouring, and native Arabs," were, on the whole, good, though a number of families of the richer sort were also of the baser, being supporters of Vichy and even of Hitler.

By Christmas 1942 the main attack on Tunis had been postponed, for neither the 1st Army nor the American forces were in a position to deliver it with that overwhelming force which alone could ensure success. Flavell urged very strongly that the Parachute Brigade he commanded should be withdrawn so that it might re-form, continue its training, and be available once more as an airborne force. His counsels and his protests fell on ears, not deaf, but forced by circumstances to be unreceptive. The general situation was such that specialists, as specialists, were at a discount. What was needed were men to thicken the line. Various plans, however, were put forward to use the Brigade in the role for which they had been trained, that of parachute troops, but they all came to nothing, mainly because to deliver airborne attacks in daylight, in exposed country dominated by the enemy from the hills from which he had not yet been dislodged, was far too costly, while to drop at night was impossible, for navigation was too uncertain in such difficult terrain, and the pilots lacked training in night flying.

By the beginning of January the Brigade had returned to Algiers, all save the 3rd Battalion, which was still involved in severe fighting. On the night of January 4th, in company with the Buffs, it attacked a position known as the Green Hill. "B" Company, advancing through "darkness shot with pink, yellow and red tracers," reached and captured a number of concrete machine-gun posts on the summit of the hill. Here they were counter-attacked by 180 Germans who advanced shoulder to shoulder, chanting war songs. They were wiped out almost to a man. The next counter-attack, however, was more successful, for "B" Company had by then run out of ammunition and were forced back to the foot of the hill. On the following day they were relieved and rejoined the remainder of the Brigade at Algiers, where they rested at the farm of St. Charles, near Boufarik, in a country of tangerine gardens and pink and red roses, with a background of blue mist and, far beyond, the faint, gracious outline of high mountains.

On January 25th the whole Brigade found themselves at Bone, whither they had been conveyed by sea. From that time onwards until the middle of April, these highly trained, specialised troops, invariably inferior to the enemy in numbers, were moved about to fill gaps as and when they occurred, and to restore the situation wherever and whenever it was necessary. "Continuous rain added to the normal discomforts of war, and the roads became so bad that for much of the time the only method of supply was by mule."

Everyone had to fight, not only the combat units but also the engineers, the signallers, the drivers, and casualties began to mount. By February 8th only seven of the officers who had originally come to North Africa with the 1st Parachute Battalion were still with it, and in the other battalions the situation was much the same.

"Whoa, Mohammed!"

It is impossible to describe this fighting in detail, but certain engagements must be mentioned. The first occurred at dawn on February 3rd, when the 1st Parachute Battalion attacked two "features," a name bestowed on any prominent hill or ridge in the landscape, called Jebel Mansour and Jebel Alliliga. Driven by heavy counter-attacks from the second of these, which all the valour of the Guards Brigade and a contingent of the Foreign Legion failed to recover, the Battalion was eventually forced back to the foot of Jebel Mansour, largely for lack of ammunition, the mules carrying it having gone astray. In this action the casualties were 183, a very high proportion of the number engaged. There was next the attack by the enemy on February 26th. The Germans advanced with the best part of two battalions but, after a fierce fight which lasted from dawn till three in the afternoon, were completely broken and tired, leaving 250 dead on the field and 150 prisoners.

It was during this fight that Lieutenant G. L. W. Street of the 3rd Battalion, going forward in the half light of dawn to visit his most advanced posts, heard a movement among the thick scrub which covered the hillside. He shouted out, calling upon the unseen men to keep quiet since there were Germans near at hand. He was immediately challenged and repeated his order. "Don't make such a . . . row," he yelled, "there may be Germans about." At that moment a German jabbed him in the stomach with a tommy gun and ordered him to lead the rest of the patrol, whom Street had mistaken for his own men, between the lines of the parachute battalion, so that they might attack its headquarters. Street led them instead to the nearest company strongpoint, where they were received with heavy fire. Fortunately Street was not hit and took cover in a fold of the ground with the German officer in command of the patrol. After a short time he turned to him and said : "Look out, my chaps are throwing grenades at us." The German officer turned his head, Street struck him a heavy blow, knocked him out, deprived him of his arms and made off to our lines. He then led some of his men in a charge which destroyed a platoon of the enemy. For these exploits he was awarded the Military Cross.

It was about this time that the Division adopted the battle-cry of "Whoa, Mohammed!" and this shout, running up and down the stony hills, roused the men to their highest endeavours and struck dismay into the hearts of the enemy. It seems to be the British soldier's imitation of the Arab's exhortation to his steed, usually a donkey.

There were next the actions fought by the Brigade in the sector north of Beja, a hundred miles away, to which they were moved at the beginning of March in a nightmare journey along roads bordered by precipices. Here they became acquainted with Jebel Abiod and the two features known as Bowler Hat and Beggars' Bump. The 3rd Battalion held a position near an iron mine, and the men, covered with its dust, assumed the colouring of Red Indians. The casualties they suffered caused the place to be named "The Death Valley."

In the very heavy fighting of the next ten days the British parachutists found themselves in combat against the élite of their German opposite numbers under the command of Colonel Witzig. These fierce and well trained troops delivered three attacks against the 2nd Battalion. The first was held fairly easily, the second with difficulty, and the third almost succeeded, when the 1st Battalion came to the rescue and saved the situation.

Man for man, the Red Devils were just a little better than Witzig's men.

Throughout these days no one distinguished himself more than Colonel Pearson, commanding the 1st Battalion, and it was at this time that he earned a bar to his D.S.O. At one moment when the fighting was particularly heavy if so happened that Down, who was by then a Brigadier, was paying a visit to the 1st Battalion, which he had once commanded. He presently found himself, armed with a rifle, fighting in the ranks and taking part in a charge of the Headquarters staff, consisting of cooks, clerks, signallers and batmen, brilliantly led by Colonel Pearson and completely successful.

The fighting round Seajenane

There was finally the fighting round Sedjenane. On March 27th, 1943, a general advance began between the sea and the level Abiod-Sedjenane road.

In forty-eight hours the parachute troops had captured not only all their objectives, together with somewhat more than 800 prisoners, but also the final objective allotted to the troops on their right, who had been held up by intense mortar fire.

At one time in this battle, Colonel Witzig's German parachutists almost restored the situation. They were posted in a wood, and for a time the efforts of the 2nd Parachute Battalion and half the third to drive them out of it were unavailing., The supply of grenades gave out, and observing this, a private soldier whose name is not recorded ran back, obtained a box, and then walked up and down the line of red berets handing out the grenades, uttering the familiar cry, "Chocolates, Cigarettes." They were used with great effect, and it was then that Lieutenant-Colonel Frost, sounding his hunting horn, led the 2nd Battalion in a bayonet charge which "obliterated the enemy."

A little farther on, the victors took prisoner an Italian Colonel with his suitcase ready packed and his batman leading his pet dog on a leash.

The adventures which befell Lieutenant-Colonel R. G. Pine-Coffin, D.S.O., M.C., and his adjutant, Captain Moore, well illustrate the nature of the fighting at this time. The 3rd

Battalion had been ordered to move west of Sedjenane and occupy the high ground. The problem facing their commanding officer was how to move his men forward in daylight up a road commanded by the enemy 's guns. To rush them up in lorries seemed the only way and they were due to start at 9.30 in the morning. Before that hour, Pine-Coffin and Moore set out in a reconnaissance vehicle, presently reaching the neighbourhood of the horseshoe-shaped hill which was to be occupied by the battalion. Here Pine-Coffin went forward to examine the position, leaving Moore lying hidden in the grass near a small Arab village in front of which stood a very "villainous-looking Arab." "Presently," records Moore, "I heard the sound of rustling, and looking up saw a Boche patrol, led by an officer, approaching. They were already in converse with the villainous-looking Arab, and I crawled behind a cactus, for I expected the Arab to tell them all about me. Either he did not know I was there or he did not choose to tell the Germans so, for they sat down and began to make tea. They remained there for half an hour, during which time I saw and heard bombing and machine-gun fire on the road behind me. I took this to mean that the battalion was on the way up.

"A short while afterwards I heard the Colonel's voice. He was shouting, 'Where are you, James?' The Boches jumped up from their tea and I thought they were certain to spot me, but presently they sat down and went on with their meal. When they had finished, they moved off, passing close to me, and went up the valley. I followed, fearing they would run into the C.O. A long burst of machine-gun fire sent me into cover again. I crawled through some bushes, and the first person I saw was the Colonel, who said, 'It looks as though the Boches are going to hold the position we've been ordered to hold.' There seemed to be a lot of Huns about." There were.

The two officers remained in a state which Moore describes as one of "awful uncertainty. We saw many figures moving about and presently discovered that they belonged to the leading company of the battalion now coming up."

The horseshoe-shaped hill was held, and they stayed there until April 14th.

A brigade of battle-seasoned men

By then the battalion was reduced to between sixty and seventy men a company. They were almost barefoot, the barrels of their rifles and Bren guns were worn, and their wireless sets were no longer serviceable. The other two battalions were in the same case, and it was with more than ordinary relief, therefore, that they welcomed the 9th American Division on the night of April 14th/15th and soon afterwards returned to Boufarik.

Here Flavell, who had been given an immediate award of the D.S.O., handed over to Brigadier G. W. Lathbury, D.S.O., M.B.E., a brigade which in three months' fighting had been awarded eight Distinguished Service Orders, fifteen Military Crosses, nine Distinguished Conduct Medals, twenty-two Military Medals, three Croix de Guerre, and one Legion of Honour.

The casualties they had suffered had been very heavy. They would have been still heavier had it not been for the gallantry and skill of the 16th Parachute Field Ambulance. These young doctors and orderlies, divided into surgical teams, dropped in every case with the fighting troops. One such team, under Lieutenant C. G. Robb, had before the end of December carried out 162 surgical operations, most of them of a severe nature, and of the men so treated only one died. Robb himself injured his knee in his first drop but concealed this fact and continued to operate for three weeks, his last patient being himself. Of these men it may be said that their courage and skill equalled those of the men whom they attended.

While it is doubtless true that to use highly trained, specialized troops to carry out such continuous, heavy fighting is extravagant, it is equally true that no others were available and that the positions had to be captured and held. One thing is certain. The 1st Parachute Brigade earned in ninety days a reputation for gallantry, discipline and initiative unsurpassed by that of any other troops in Africa. They were soon to be joined by the remainder of the Airborne Division, who were to take part in the next stage of the Mediterranean campaign.

CHAPTER 6

THE NEXT ACT IS REHEARSED

ALL THROUGH 1942 the Commander of the Airborne Forces and his staff had been struggling with three main difficulties, shortage of men, deficiency of equipment and lack of aircraft. To take them in order : very many of the men who had just completed their training had had to be sent to North Africa to replace the casualties suffered by the 1st Parachute Brigade. The ranks of the 2nd, from which they were perforce drawn, were therefore much depleted, and this in turn affected the formation of the 3rd. Such necessary auxiliary services as Engineers, Signals and Medical Corps were also much below strength. Recruiting for these and for the Parachute Battalions was a matter of difficulty, for only the most efficient type of soldier could be considered, and commanding officers were, not unnaturally, reluctant to encourage their best men to volunteer. There was, too, a shortage of glider pilots, mainly owing to training difficulties, and the Glider Pilot Regiment had sustained a grievous loss by the death in October 1942 of Colonel Rock, killed in a glider which crashed during a night-landing experiment. The first to help in the creation of the new force, he had been throughout unsparing of himself, and he must be included in that select company of Englishmen, little known to their fellow-countrymen as a whole, who have rendered inestimable service and taken no heed of the cost.

Vital items of equipment were also scarce or, to use a curious specimen of modern English, "in short supply." It had long been decided that jeeps must be the basic transport of the Division. By the beginning of 1943, 132 of these vehicles had not yet come to hand. They "were reported to be standing on a quayside waiting to be delivered, but it could not be discovered on which side 'of the Atlantic this quay side was.'" There were too few six-pounder anti-tank and twenty-mm. Hispano guns, and there were no reserves for the Tetrarch tank designed to be carried by the Hamilcar glider.

To crown all, a suitable form of wireless set was yet to be forthcoming.

As with men and equipment, so with aircraft. The numbers available for No. 38 Wing were considerably below the numbers required. Only half an Air Landing Battalion could be carried at one time, and no tugs capable of towing a fully loaded Horsa any length of distance had yet made their appearance. This lack of aircraft put a heavy brake on training, particularly on the training of the glider-borne troops who were now beginning to come forward in considerable numbers. It seemed hard to avoid the conclusion that the Royal Air Force Wing detailed to carry airborne forces was the Cinderella of the Service. All through 1942 the most strenuous efforts were being made to equip Bomber Command with a large and efficient number of aircraft, and to perform a similar service for airborne troops was beyond the productive capacities of the country at that moment. The situation was relieved by our American Allies, who were willing and able to place a considerable number of Dakotas at our disposal. They were suitable both for parachuting and for towing gliders, but their crews, though keen and determined, lacked training.

This may seem a gloomy picture, but there were compensations ; the chief was the high heart of the officers and men. The exploits of the 1st Parachute Brigade in North Africa had had a great effect on those who had still to go into action and who were resolved to equal, and to surpass if they could, the achievements of their predecessors.

Problems of the Sicily planners

At the beginning of 1943 the Divisional Commander was informed, somewhat to his consternation, that his troops would be required to proceed overseas almost immediately and be ready for action against the enemy by midsummer. Norman, who had already visited the 1st Parachute Brigade in North Africa and returned, his mind full of the lessons learnt during their campaign, went a second time to Tunisia and on to the Middle East, to discover what part the Airborne Division could play in operations then being planned against Sicily and due to take place in June or July. He was accompanied by Brigadier Hopkinson, and both men soon discovered that the planners on the spot regarded the participation of airborne forces as indispensable.

The attack on Sicily would, it was realized, certainly prove a complicated and difficult business for the Navy and the seaborne troops in their charge.

It would be even more so for those who were to be airborne. . They would have to fly 350 miles, partly over sea, in a semi-tropical climate, to find in all probability their landing disputed by the enemy, and, an added complication, they must travel in a type of aircraft and of glider to which their training had not accustomed them. The parachutists would have to leap from a door, not drop through a hole, while the other troops would be passengers in Hadrian gliders, usually known by their American name, Waco. They hold at most eighteen men, as compared with the thirty-two carried in the Horsas.

The Dakotas were not powerful enough to tow the heavier glider the required distance.

In view of the shortage of trained American glider pilots it was felt essential that a sufficient number of officers and men of the Glider Pilot Regiment, who had either completed their training or were well advanced in it, should as soon as possible be brought up to the standard required for operations against the enemy. The regiment, now under the command of Chatterton, who had taken Rock's place on his death, was accordingly ordered at short notice to North Africa, where it arrived at the end of April 1943. Its officers and men found that they had exchanged the comparative comfort of Salisbury Plain for two airfields in the Mascara area of Algeria, both of which had been condemned by the French as too badly infected with malaria to be serviceable. It says much for the physical fitness and mental stamina of the glider pilots, and the pilots and crews of the American Air Force tugs who accompanied them and worked with them, that, during the whole period of training, sickness from all causes was almost nil.

Difficulties were many, but they were all overcome. Most of the pilots had never flown a Waco, and none of them were able to do so between the hours of ten in the morning and five in the evening because of the great heat, which made conditions in the cockpits insupportable. Moreover, the Wacos had not been unpacked, and the first task was to erect them. Though they lacked all previous experience, the pilots set to and assembled fifty-two in ten days.

Chatterton concentrated the attention of his first pilots on learning how to take off quickly and easily- in formation and, above all, how to land both in moonlight and in darkness. The training of the second pilots was devoted to map reading, pin-pointing and general navigation, and also to manipulating the trimming tabs of the glider and the "spoilers," a special apparatus fitted to enable the speed of the Waco to be checked.

A fourteen-hundred-mile tow

It presently became evident that a certain number of Horsa gliders would have to be used. The main disadvantage of the Waco is that it is not large enough to take both a jeep and what it is required to tow, an anti-tank gun.

Separated, the uses of both are limited ; together they form a mobile and effective combination. If Wacos alone were available against Sicily, the jeep and the gun would have to be carried not in one glider but in two, and it was impossible to guarantee that both would arrive at the same spot at the same time. The Horsa, however, was large enough to transport the combination. The question was, how could a sufficient number be brought to North Africa. They were both large and fragile, and this made their transport by ship difficult. Moreover, they would occupy space in which heavier and more urgent cargo could be stowed. Whether they could be towed all the way from this country seemed more than doubtful, till Group Captain Cooper, ever foremost in exploring new technical possibilities, testing new devices and encouraging others to follow his example, with Squadron Leader Wilkinson, proved by a series of flights round England that a Halifax could tow an unloaded Horsa 1,400 miles and still land with a small reserve of fuel. At the end of April orders were accordingly issued for Halifaxes to tow Horsas to the airfield of Sale, not far from Casablanca in French Morocco, and to have them there by the end of July. They were then to be towed to Kairouan in Tunisia and finally, when the operation began, to Sicily. As things turned out, the period of time allotted for covering the first lap was too short, but only by a week. The task was formidable enough. Each Halifax had to fly about seventy hours, of which fifty were spent in towing. They were very heavily loaded, extra petrol being carried in the bomb bays, which meant that a forced landing with wheels up would almost inevitably cause the aircraft to burst into flames. This indeed happened on the only occasion when such a landing had to be made.

The flights were carried out in daylight, for it was thought to be too risky to fly at night, lest the tug should enter cloud, be lost to view, or encounter turbulent air and put so great a strain on the tow rope that it would part.

In daylight, not cloud but hostile aircraft were the danger; for, since to carry enough petrol to fly far out over the Atlantic was impossible, the route ran within a hundred miles of the enemy's air bases in south-western France.

One day a Halifax with its tug encountered two Focke-Wulf Condors which were returning from a raid on a convoy off Portugal. In the fight which ensued, the Halifax was shot down and the glider released. It fell into the sea; the three pilots on board took to their dinghy, and were rescued eleven days later by a passing Spanish ship. Another tug and glider, reaching the same area a day or two later, disappeared and have never been heard of again. Major A. J. Cooper, a glider pilot, had a most alarming experience. The tow parted and the glider landed in the sea. He was alone and took to his dinghy, in which he spent ten hours before being picked up and brought back to England. Knowing how short-handed was the Glider Pilot Regiment, he lost no time in seeking recovery from the effects of this accident by resting, but within twenty-four hours was once more at the controls of a glider and this time arrived safely in North Africa. He lost his life soon afterwards in the Sicilian expedition.

Despite all the difficulties of distance, weather and enemy action, more than eighty per cent. of the Horsas thus ferried to Africa arrived. Once at Sale, the next stage of their journey was a distance of 350 miles to the aerodrome at Froha. Here the main difficulty was the bumpy nature of the passage, for it was not possible to take off in the early morning-a time of day when in those parts there is much low cloud. Two gliders parted from their tugs on this stage of the journey, possibly because of the rough air, and landed in the desert. One of them was recovered in time for the operation.

The final stage was perhaps the most difficult of all. The tugs and gliders had to fly from Froha to Kairouan, and had therefore to cross mountains which rise as high as 7,000 feet. "I used to fly at 9,000 feet," reported Flight Lieutenant D. A. Grant, pilot of one of the tugs. "Some pilots flew lower, even at 6,500 feet, along the valley. This was all right if one got there early in the morning, but later in the day one could lose as much as 1,300 feet in one bump. During my last trip l lost about 3,000 feet over a period of ten minutes. This was an extremely tiring trip for the pilots.

It involved a long climb at a hundred feet a minute to 9,000 feet, and either a very bumpy journey if they started late, or an hour and a half flying dead into the morning sun." The first glider reached Kairouan on June 28th, twelve days before the invasion of Sicily began.

Strenuous days of training

While tug crews and the pilots of gliders were thus making ready, the remainder of the Division had not been idle. By the end of May it was concentrated in the Mascara area, where it got into immediate touch with No. 51 Wing of the American troop-carrying Command, which was to provide nearly all the air transport for the invasion. Camps were established near the airfields, and the Divisional stores landed at Oran gradually arrived by rail. "In this case the performance of the Algerian railways, always eccentric, was complicated by a change of gauge halfway, at a place called Perregaux. It was also soon discovered that stores left unguarded on the railway did not arrive at their destination."

By the first week in June the troops who were to travel in the gliders, and who composed the Air Landing Brigade, had begun their training in a part of the world composed largely of a vast plain of "red clay soil surrounded by mountainous, desolate country . . . . The climate was hot and becoming hotter, and the dust was already a considerable nuisance; but the local wine was discovered to be plentiful, cheap, crude and surprisingly strong."

In these conditions the Brigade, under its commander, Brigadier P. H. W. Hicks, D.S.O., M.C., found itself leading a strenuous existence. "During the day there was usually sufficient wind to create a continuous fine rain of red dust, and this became a soft wall whenever an aircraft took off. To take off in a glider in these conditions was a considerable experience, as, until it was off the ground, all that could be seen was the tow rope disappearing into a thick wall of red dust, through which the tug finally appeared long after the glider had left the airfield." The local Arab population maintained "a constant and exhausted indifference to anything except money and material gain." At the outset, the French inhabitants were suspicious and covertly hostile, but this attitude changed as time went on and they began to remember that they belonged to a country the vast majority of whose citizens nourished implacable hatred for their temporary conquerors.

The training of the parachute troops continued side by side with that of the Air Landing Brigade and was equally strenuous. Altogether, from May 8th to June 30th, 8,913 jumps were made. By then the plans for the invasion of Sicily had assumed their final shape and preparations for the enterprise were almost complete.

Two months before the expedition set out the Airborne troops had suffered a second and most grievous loss. On May 20th, 1943, Nigel Norman, by then an Air Commodore and Air Officer commanding No. 38 Wing, took off from England with his staff in a Lockheed Hudson bound for North Africa, there to take part in the planning. About an hour and a half later one of the instruments developed a defect which made a return to base inevitable.

The Hudson landed, the repair was made, and the party took off once more.

The aircraft had flown only a mile or two, and was but a few hundred feet up, when the port engine failed. At that moment Norman was standing in the cockpit between the first and second pilots. He at once returned to the body of the aircraft and ordered everyone to brace himself as firmly as possible, against the inevitable forced landing. Having seen them take up their positions, he flung himself on the portable bed, the only place available, the other and safer stations being occupied. The Hudson struck the ground and Norman was flung violently against its side, breaking his neck and dying immediately. Of the others on board, all were injured, the wireless operator fatally, but they succeeded in climbing out of the aircraft, which almost immediately burst into flames. Had they not received that last-minute warning, more, perhaps all, of them would almost certainly have been killed.

So died Nigel Norman, to whose vision and steadfastness of purpose the Airborne Forces owe so much. "Why must you always want a hundred per cent?" a high officer once peevishly inquired of him. His reply is not recorded, but the history of his country supplies it. England has been always fortunate in her pioneers, whose genius and determination have so often secured her victory, and whose example, if she is to live, must ever inspire her sons.

CHAPTER 7

BATTLE FOR THE SICILIAN BRIDGES

THE AIRBORNE ATTACK against the Axis forces in Sicily consisted of four operations, two carried out by British and two by American troops. With the last two this account is not concerned for it is confined to a description of what befell the British airborne forces during the war. The first operation took place on the night of July 9th/10th. It was carried out entirely by glider-borne troops. Their object was to secure the Ponte Grande, a very important bridge near Syracuse, and to attack the western outskirts of that city with the object of creating a diversion so as to ease the task of the seaborne forces. The first British Air Landing Brigade consisting of two battalions with anti tank guns sappers and a medical unit, were to be carried in 129 Wacos and eight Horsa gliders towed by 109 Dakotas flown by American pilots and seven Halifaxes and twenty one Albemarles belonging to the Royal Air Force. The tugs were not to approach the coast nearer than 3,000 yards and were to release the gliders between 9.10 and 10.30 p.m., the Wacos at 1,900 feet and the Horsas at 4,000. The first were to land in zones west of the Maddalena Peninsula on the southern side of the great harbour where an Athenian fleet had met destruction more than twenty three centuries before the second in fields north of the canal bridge half way up the western side of the harbour The ground chosen for all landing zones was partly cultivated partly pasture and thickly strewn with orchards.

To fly direct from Kairouan to Sicily might mean that the force would be picked up by the radio-location instruments of the enemy. This risk, it was decided, should not be accepted. A devious route was therefore followed, the gliders and tugs making for Delimara Point on the south-east coast of Malta, and then turning north-east towards Sicily, passing Cape Passero, and thence on to the neighbourhood of Cap Murro di Porco. Two and a half miles short of this promontory the gliders were to be released. The Halifaxes, which were to tow the Horsas, had only reached Kairouan three days before, and the crews were kept very busy preparing and guarding their aircraft, digging slit trenches, " manhandling fifty-gallon barrels of petrol, and erecting tents."

At one o'clock in the afternoon of July 9th the special briefing of the pilots of each combination took place. Every Horsa was to carry thirty-two men of the South Staffordshire Regiment together with their equipment, which included Bangalore torpedoes to be used for the destruction of barbed wire. The number of men in the Wacos varied according to the amount of equipment on board. The maximum number was eighteen armed only with their personal weapons, the minimum four with a jeep. The men on board the Wacos came from the 1st Border Regiment, the 2nd South Staffordshire Regiment, the 9th Field Company, Royal Engineers, and the 181st Airborne Field Ambulance. All were under the command of Brigadier Hicks. Six airfields were used for the take-off", the first combination becoming airborne at 6.48 p.m.

A rough passage to Sicily

At the last moment bad weather nearly wrecked the expedition. A strong south-easterly wind sprang up which caused a number of the combinations to be blown oh" course, especially on the second leg after they had left Malta.

The strength of the gale reached at times forty-live m.p.h., and, since the wind was on the quarter most of the way to Malta, flying conditions were very rough. Moreover, it was necessary to fly low to escape detection by radiolocation. So low indeed

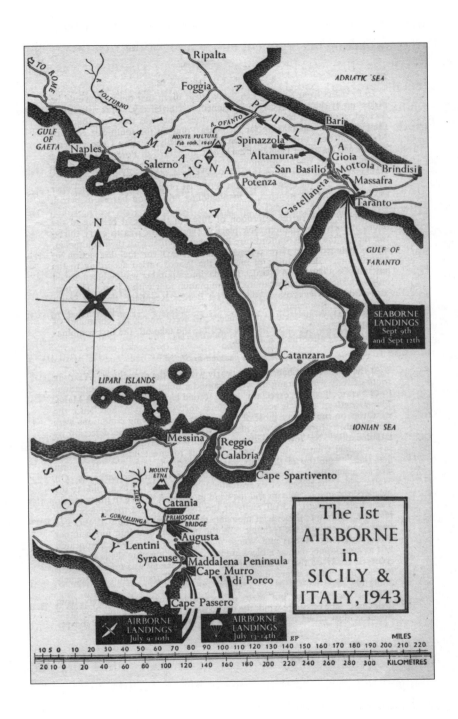

TO ROME

Ripalta

R. VOLTURNO

Foggia

ADRIATIC SEA

A P U L I A

R. OFANTO

Bari

GULF OF GAETA

MONTE VULTURE
Feb 10th 1941

Spinazzola

Naples

CAMPAGNA

Altamura

Gioia

Salerno

San Basilio

Mottola

Brindisi

Massafra

Potenza

Castellaneta

Taranto

I T A L Y

GULF OF TARANTO

SEABORNE
LANDINGS
Sept 9th
and Sept 12th

N

Catanzara

LIPARI ISLANDS

IONIAN SEA

Messina

Reggio
Calabria

Cape Spartivento

MOUNT ETNA

R. SIMETO

Catania

R. GORNALUNGA

PRIMOSOLE
BRIDGE

S I C I L Y

Lentini

Augusta

Syracuse

Maddalena Peninsula

Cape Murro
di Porco

Cape Passero

AIRBORNE
LANDINGS
July 9-10th

AIRBORNE
LANDINGS
July 13-14th

The 1st
AIRBORNE
in
SICILY &
ITALY, 1943

EP

MILES

10 5 0   10   20   30   40   50   60   70   80   90   100   110   120   130   140   150   160   170   180   190   200   210   220

20 10 0   20   40   60   80   100   120   140   160   180   200   220   240   260   280   300   KILOMETRES

were the airborne invaders that at Malta, says Colonel Chatterton who was taking his regiment into action for the first time, " the top of the cliffs was level with the gliders." The storm was such that the breakers could clearly be seen, despite the darkness. OH Malta, where the swords of six searchlights pierced the sky as a guide to the invaders, the moon came up and the wind moderated, falling to thirty m.p.h.

The whole force arrived off Sicily at the right time, and the gliders were released. This was the crucial moment, the culminating point of weeks of hasty, hard, enthusiastic training. By the pale light of a thin moon in her first quarter, the Horsas and Wacos made for the shore, which appeared first as a dark line, then as a black smudge. A few bursting shells and some coloured tracer on the horizon showed that the enemy was uneasy, though whether he was fully aware of what was about to fall upon him was extremely doubtful.

The releases began, but many gliders were parted prematurely from their tugs. The off-shore wind, the darkness of the night, enhanced by great clouds of dust raised by the wind from the arid Sicilian shore, the inexperience of the tug pilots, all contributed to this mistake, which was to have serious consequences and might well have proved fatal to success. It is impossible to tell the story of each individual glider, but some of the more striking incidents must be recorded. Chatterton, with Brigadier Hicks on board, was one of those pilots whose gliders were released too far off.

He realized that he would be unable to make the shore, and so steered for a black patch which loomed ahead, hoping that it was a small island on the sea. He had almost reached it when a stream of tracer bullets came from its summit, a searchlight was turned on and he perceived himself to be approaching a steep cliff. He put the glider into a right-handed stalling turn and plunged seawards. At that moment his starboard wing was hit and damaged, the glider struck the waves, and its occupants began to claw their way out. Only one of them was injured, but they were in a sorry plight, a mile from the shore, illuminated by a searchlight, and under intermittent but heavy machine-gun fire. "All is not well, Bill," Brigadier Hicks was heard to murmur to his Brigade-Major as he crawled on to the uninjured wing. In the circumstances his remark was not exaggerated.

The pilots and their passengers lay or crouched on the wing watching other gliders making for the shore. Many did not reach it, but like their own fell into the sea. Soon sounds of battle were heard on the coast, accompanied by the flash of tracer. Chatterton, Hicks and the rest decided to swim for it.

Leaving the wrecked and water-logged glider, they struck out for the beach, reached it eventually and there, falling in with a party who had been more fortunate than themselves and were on their way to dispose of a coastal battery, at length arrived at the Headquarters of the Airborne Force.

The reports of the glider pilots, and of some of their passengers on that night of wind and storm, show how perilous was the task and how great the determination to fulfil it. "Good but bumpy tow, glider almost uncontrollable for live minutes over Malta owing to bad weather ...."

"Glider just missed reaching land owing to a hundred-foot cliff ...."

"Owing to strong wind pilot unable to make land and landed in sea about 600 yards from coast ...."

"Glider released over sea- distance off-shore unknown - landed in sea approximately three or four miles off-shore-all missing with the exception of two passengers ...."

"Successful and accurate tow under bumpy conditions-glider released and made successful landing half mile east of correct landing zone ...."

"Glider landed on beach fifty yards from sea close to enemy post-ammunition hand-cart in glider exploded, believed caused by enemy grenade thrown into glider-two men wounded, eight missing ...."

"Very good tow, glider released about one mile off-shore and landed in field next to landing zone ...."

"Rough flight, glider subjected to A.A. fire after release, heavy tracer, left wing hit, Hew over landing zone and landed sixteen miles south-west of Syracuse, hitting a six-foot wall-left wing burning, also seventy-seven grenades ignited inside glider, thick smoke in glider and men trapped by ammunition panniers which began to explode-intense heat and small arms fire made extrication of men difficult-two pilots and twelve other ranks killed, seven wounded."

Not many of the gliders which succeeded in making Sicily reached the designated landing zones. Some came down as much as forty miles away.

Captain I. McArthur, for example, came in to land in pitch darkness over country intersected with stone walls. At the last moment he saw a field of stubble, but as he was about to touch down on it, his undercarriage struck a wall, the glider landed on its nose and he broke his left foot. The men on board released him and his second pilot, also injured, made them comfortable in a ditch and then set out for their objective. They all reached it.

The Horsas towed by the Halifaxes were hardly more fortunate. Only one came down successfully on the landing zone ; of the rest, three landed some two miles away, and one carrying Bangalore torpedoes was hit by anti-aircraft fire and blew up in the air; Glider No. 133, whose pilot was Staff Sergeant Galpin, and which had on board Lieutenant L. Withers and his platoon, was the only one to land on the chosen spot near the Ponte Grande.

They wasted no time awaiting the arrival of the rest, but advanced immediately to attack the bridge. Lieutenant Withers and five men swam the canal and made for an enemy pill-box at the northern end of the bridge, while the rest of the platoon put in an attack from the south. In less than half an hour the bridge was captured without loss to the attacking forces, who, after removing demolition charges and cutting telephone wires, settled down to the task of defending it against the inevitable counter-attacks.

The bitter struggle for the Ponte Grande

They were reinforced at dawn by seven men from the advanced platoon of the 1st Airborne Brigade, who arrived just in time to take part in the repelling of a determined counter-attack by three armoured cars, one of which lost its commanding officer. Soon afterwards, Lieutenant-Colonel A. G. Walch, O.B.E., appeared and took over command of the defence. By half-past six in the morning seven officers and eighty other ranks were maintaining it, with the aid, in addition to their small arms, of one three-inch and one two-inch mortar, with only a few rounds of ammunition, mostly smoke, four Bren machine-guns and a single gammon bomb. The defence was soon subjected to heavy and accurate mortar fire to which, for lack of ammunition, they could make only an inadequate reply. The bridge was also shelled at intervals by a field gun. Men were soon hit; at 9 a.m. the Second-in-Command was killed, and all through that morning casualties mounted steadily.

By a quarter to three in the afternoon the outlying posts had been wiped out and the defensive position enfiladed. Half an hour later, of the original force only fifteen remained unwounded and these were "cornered at the point where the canal joins the sea and where there was no cover whatsoever."

Another quarter of an hour passed, and then "the force, having almost exhausted its ammunition, was over-run by the enemy."

But their splendid defence had not been in vain. The enemy had no materials with which to destroy the bridge he had with such difficulty regained.

Not three-quarters of an hour after the last of the glider-borne troops had been killed or captured, patrols of an Infantry Brigade which had landed from the sea arrived in the area. There they met with Lieutenant Welch and seven men who had eluded the fate of their comrades. An attack to regain the bridge was at once launched, and in a few minutes the leading elements of the Royal Scots Fusiliers had won back everything which the gallantry of the South Staffordshires had originally taken. Such of these as had survived, wounded and unwounded, had in the meantime been marched westwards towards the interior of the island; They had not gone far when they were rescued by one of our patrols which took their captors prisoner. In this fashion was the all-important bridge taken, lost and retaken. The success thus more than justified the hazards of the operation.

Alarm, confusion and dismay

But this was by no means all. Other actions fought that day by glider-borne troops greatly assisted the 8th Army during those most perilous hours of an invasion, the period when the troops are coming ashore. Two incidents may be mentioned. Waco Glider No. 10, containing part of Brigade Headquarters with Colonel O. L. Jones, Deputy Commander, landed very close to a coastal battery. They were alone, for no other gliders made their appearance. Deciding that the quantity and disposition of the barbed wire surrounding the battery defences made it too strong to be attacked at night, the small party lay up in a farmyard nearby and waited for dawn. When the sun came up, this band of Staff officers, signallers and glider pilots went up against the battery in a most careful-and well-organised manner. The Staff officers showed especial resolution, for they were putting into practice the principles they had so often preached. At 11.15 a.m. the battery was attacked and neither the rifle fire nor the grenades of the garrison sufficed to defend it. It was very soon over-run; five field guns were destroyed and the ammunition dump blown up.

While those in Waco glider No. 10 were thus acquitting themselves, a party of the 2nd South Staffordshire Regiment, carried in glider No. 7, landed in the sea 250 yards from the shore. They reached it after a time by swimming under heavy fire, and in so doing suffered a number of casualties.

From their ranks three officers, a medical officer and his orderly and a signal-man were able eventually to join their battalion. To do so they crawled through twenty feet of barbed wire, marched ten 'miles and reported for duty in the evening, having captured two pill-boxes, twenty-one prisoners, three machine guns and an anti-tank gun on the way.

These small but hard-fought engagements, typical of those which took place that night of July 9th and the day following, spread alarm, confusion and dismay among the ranks of the Italian garrison in Syracuse and the neighbourhood. Of that there is no doubt. Despite the fact that, out of 108 gliders fifty fell into the sea, and twenty-five more were never seen or heard of again, the operation must be deemed successful. On this point General Sir Bernard Montgomery, as he then was, had no doubt at all. Though the airborne operation had proved more difficult than had been expected, the main objective, the Ponte Grande, that great bridge key to the advance northward, had been captured and held. "For those responsible for this particular operation," said the General in his message to the Air Landing Brigade, "I am filled with admiration. Others who by their initiative fought isolated actions in various parts of the battle field have played no small part in this most successful landing action. Had it not been for the skill and gallantry of the Air Landing Brigade the port of Syracuse would not have fallen until very much later."

Next objective - Primosole Bridge

In the next operation the 1st Parachute Brigade was once more given a chance to show its mettle Within forty eight hours of the invasion of Sicily the 8th Army was firmly established in

Syracuse and on the march north wards towards Catania of which the capture would give the Allies control over most of eastern Sicily. Catania is a port situated on the coastal plain backed by a range of mountains, of which the pride is the volcano of Etna. To reach it from Syracuse it is necessary to cross a number of hills and then to descend on to a plain well cultivated and traversed by numerous irrigation channels .Through this plain runs the river Simeto which enters the sea about six miles south of Catania. The main road from Syracuse crosses the river a little to the east of its junction with the Gornalunga Canal by means of a bridge called Primosole. To secure it would make possible the immediate advance of the 8th Army moving down from the high ground south of Catania and would as at Syracuse shorten the campaign. It was decided therefore that the three Parachute Battalions under their tried and trusted leaders Lieutenant Colonels Pearson, Frost and Yeldham, should drop on four dropping zones to the west of the bridge two near the river which there winds sinuously to the sea and two near the comparatively straight canal. The Parachute battalions were to be assisted in their task by men of the 1st Parachute Squadron of the Royal Engineers under Major Murray and by an Airborne Anti Tank Unit of the 'P A under Major Arnold The 16th Paratroop Field Ambulance was also included.

The plan was for two platoons of the 1st Parachute Battalion and the Squadron of Royal Engineers to seize the objective by coup de main, while two platoons of the 3rd dropping five minutes later should over run a four gun anti aircraft battery near by which was expected to give trouble. The remainder of the 1st Parachute Battalion would then organise the defence of the bridge and the remainder of the 3rd would establish a bridgehead in a loop of the Simeto 1,000 yards to the north of Primosole while the 2nd Battalion would hold the high ground south of the bridge. The Brigade was under the command of Brigadier Lathbury and was to be carried to its destination the parachute troops in 105 Dakotas from the American Troop Carrier Command and eleven Albemarles of the R.A.F., the glider borne troops in eight Waco gliders and eleven Horsas towed by Halifaxes and Albemarles.

The Brigade entered the waiting aircraft on the same six airfields near Kairouan from which their glider borne comrades had set out four nights before. At first all went well. The number of aircraft which failed, owing to last minute mishaps, to leave the ground was very small ; soon the Force was on its way flying a course which brought it over the Kuriate Isles to Malta, and thence north-east past Syracuse and Augusta to the dropping zones. On approaching Sicily when in the neighbourhood of Cape Passero and Cape Murro di Porco, already known to many of the pilots who had taken part in the previous operation, a misfortune occurred which jeopardized and might have ruined the expedition.

The Force flies into bad luck

Anti-aircraft fire, varying in intensity, but some of it heavy, was opened by Allied naval forces on the American Dakotas and the British Albemarles and Halifaxes. Considerable damage was caused and a number of aircraft shot down. In all fairness this mishap must be attributed for the most part to the fortunes of war. The enemy's Air Force had been operating sporadically over the beach-heads, and the naval gun crews were agog to defend their ships and the craft plying to the shore and back. To blame them for being too eager, too quick on the trigger, is easy but unjust. Aircraft recognition, at all times difficult, was especially so that night, for there was haze over the coast. Moreover, no small proportion of the transport aircraft were off course and flying in the danger zone, a belt five miles wide running along the coast of Sicily. To experience anti-aircraft tire is always unpleasant, to say the least of it, and when flying an unarmed and unarmoured Dakota with no self-sealing tanks, it is more than usually so.

This fire from friendly vessels and presently from the enemy's, anti-aircraft guns, whose crews could see their targets in the bright moonlight the haze did not extend inland-caused confusion as well as casualties.

Evasive action was taken in some instances over the dropping zones, and more than one parachute soldier, standing ready to cast himself into the void, was flung to the floor of the aircraft and, becoming entangled in his static line, was unable to jump. Disorder in the air meant confusion on the ground ; the assembling of the Brigade at the rendezvous near the dropping zones did not take place according to plan.

During the first phase of the action, which lasted from the moment of dropping soon after 10 p.m. on the 13th, to dawn on the 14th, officers and men of the three Parachute Battalions were for the most part engaged in trying to find each other in the darkness and then in discovering the whereabouts of the bridge they were to attack. By 2.15 in the morning, however, Captain Rann and fifty men of the 1st Parachute Battalion had attacked the bridge from the north and secured it, meeting with little opposition. A little later, the Brigade Commander arrived on the spot, but was wounded by a grenade "thrown by a stray Italian." The charges in the bridge were removed and thrown into the river, and preparations for defending the position were made. Dawn broke upon 120 men of the 1st Parachute Battalion and two platoons of the 3rd established at the bridge with two three-inch mortars, one Vickers machine-gun and three Piats - those useful, indeed indispensable, anti-tank weapons.

The difficulties of landing, forming up and collecting the equipment dropped in the containers had been increased by the fact, unknown before the expedition set out, that German parachute troops had just landed on some of the same dropping zones to reinforce the garrisons in the neighbourhood. One of our men, returning to open a container, was approached by a dimly seen figure who enquired of him in German whether he had found his "Schmeisser." These Germans, were stout troops, the Italians less so.

Major P. Young, who made a heavy landing and broke his leg, was being attended to by two members of this "stick," when some fifty Italian soldiers appeared. They showed no kind of light but undertook, while the uninjured parachutists went off to their objective, to surrender to Major Young and look after him. This they did.

Adventures of an anti-tank battery

The anti-tank battery of the Light Regiment of the Royal Artillery carried in gliders had many adventures. Most of the gliders successfully reached shore, where the landing zones were clearly visible. That they could be so easily seen was due, as Staff Sergeant White, one of the pilots, reported, to the enemy's anti-aircraft fire which with its flaming tracer shells and bullets was far brighter than the landing lights set out by the markers of the Independent Parachute Company now acting as Pathfinders for the first time. The flak was indeed intense. The 'glider carrying part of "D" troop, for example, which landed north-east of Lentini, was riddled with bullets in the air, but they caused only one casualty. A glider carrying a section of "A" troop fell into the river and all its occupants save one were killed or injured.

Another carrying the Battery Headquarters crashed with even graver results, for no one on board escaped death or injury Sergeant White's Horsa was more fortunate. He arrived over the landing zone at 1,500 feet twenty seven minutes late circled through the fire and landed successfully without casualties only a hundred yards south of the bridge. His cargo, a gun and jeep though it took a considerable time to unload them were both in action the following day as were those of Lieutenant Thomas's Horsa which landed successfully in a ravine seven miles from the objective.

At dawn all who had reached the rendezvous were established in two positions the larger number being at the bridge the smaller on the high ground a mile south of it This had been captured three hours earlier after a brief fight with small arms and hand grenades. Its defence was organised by Major R T H Lonsdale who had under him 120 men including twenty signallers without wireless and no heavy weapons. At 6.30 in the morning he was attacked by German parachute troops and heavily shelled by mortars of the Light Regiment, who was in wireless communication with a British six-inch gun cruiser lying off shore. The aid he was able to furnish was timely for by mid morning Lonsdale and his men were hard pressed since the enemy made no attempt to close, but remained out of the effective range of his light machine-guns, and continued to drop mortar bombs in great profusion and with considerable effect upon the exposed position. The cruiser opened fire and her broadsides of six-inch shells soon quietened or put an end to the activity of a number of mortars, machine-guns and snipers, drove the enemy out of a number of nearby buildings destroyed two guns of a coastal battery and set on fire its ammunition.

Meanwhile all was reasonably quiet at the bridge itself where Italians emerging from burning houses were still surrendering in driblets 9.30 contact by wireless was established for about half an hour with a British armoured unit, subsequently found to be the 4th Armoured Brigade, pushing up the road from distant Syracuse with intent to relieve the parachute troops.

Its Commander reported that he was not yet able to do so, the message faded during transmission, and no further signals were picked up. As the morning wore on, it was evident that the enemy was massing for a counter-attack in force. It was delivered at lunch-time under cover of smoke and supported by fighter aircraft, and was repulsed. At 2 p.m. a much heavier an attack was made. This, too, was held, but with some difficulty, and the perimeter around the bridge was shortened.

The defence was assisted by three guns of the Light Regiment served by Sergeants Anderson, Atkinson and Doig, who had by then reached the bridge. They were presently joined by an officer who instructed the glider pilots in faction with the troops how to load and fire two enemy anti-tank guns on the bridge. A fourth gun might also have been present had it not landed too far to the north on the outer defences of the Catania airfield.

Its crew immobilised it under fire and subsequently withdrew to the bridge, where they manned a captured eighty-eight mm. gun. After the failure of the second counter-attack the enemy shelled the parachute troops with self-propelled guns, infantry support guns firing shrapnel, and anti-aircraft weapons. The first and second attacks had come from the south. For the third, however, the enemy's infantry appeared at the northern end of the bridge, and by five o'clock had forced those who held it to withdraw to pill-boxes on the southern bank of the river.

The position of the Brigade was now serious and was soon to become critical. It was beginning to suffer severely from that malady most dreaded by parachute troops, shortage of ammunition. Yet they still held and were able to make good use of Italian Breda machine-guns captured that morning.

The situation grew worse and worse throughout the long, hot afternoon.

By now, anti-tank guns were engaging the pill-boxes, and enemy infantry had crossed the river to the east of the bridge. The parachute soldiers then found themselves in danger of being smoked out, for the cornfields and rushes, their only cover, were burning. By seven o'clock in the evening the bridge was being swept by rifle and machine-gun fire at fairly close range, and attacks were coming in simultaneously from the north, the east and the south. The Brigade, under its wounded but indomitable Commander, was faced with the alternatives of withdrawing towards Major Lonsdale's position, if he and it still existed-there had been no communication with him for many hours-or of remaining where they were without ammunition and with no prospect, therefore, of continuing the fight.

The bridge is lost and recaptured

It was decided to withdraw in small parties, and this the defenders did.

"We went back and I got hit in the back of the neck," says Corporal Stanion, who was at the northern end of the bridge and gives a vivid account of the action at this stage. "I was knocked out for some length of time. When I came to, I saw a couple of German machine-gunners in the ditch where our troops should have been. A shell burst in front of me and under cover of this I ran back to the bridge. The battalion had gone. Some Italians I met with tried to explain that they had gone over to the other side. I could not cross the bridge because it was under fire, so I went into the reeds and there ran into some Jerries and was captured. I sat there for an hour or two while they argued amongst themselves as to who was to take me backs! Then apparently our chaps started firing into the reeds. Two jerries got hit in the head straight away. The others ran back and I crawled along through the reeds, which were smouldering in parts. I got down to a point where they went into the water, into which I slipped and dog-paddled over to the other side, where I lay. I was in full view of both sides and feared that, if I tried to identify myself, I would be shot. It was then about 4.30 in the afternoon. I lay there waiting for darkness to come."

Unknown to the hard-pressed airborne troops, help was at hand. The first tanks of the 4th Armoured Brigade were beginning to reach Lonsdale's position soon after dark. At midnight they were reinforced, and a company of the Durham Light Infantry arrived. Of all this, however, Brigadier Lathbury was ignorant, for he was not able to get into contact with Lonsdale 's forces until dawn on the following day, July 15th. He therefore spent a night of great mental anxiety and greater physical pain, well aware that he and his men had done all they could to hold the bridge, but tormented by the thought that they were no longer able to do so.

At six o'clock his anxiety turned to joy, for he learnt that the tanks had arrived. Even then all was not well, for the attack launched by the Durham Light Infantry, supported by the tanks, was driven back with heavy casualties. By then the Brigadier, overcome by his Wounds, had to seek medical aid, and was taken off to the dressing station. The rest of the day was marked by intermittent artillery tire from both sides, but no further attempt to retake the bridge was made until six o "clock on the morning of July 16th, when the Durham Light Infantry, guided across the river by Lieutenant-

Colonel Pearson, commanding the 1st Parachute Battalion, an officer and a sergeant, advanced to the attack, reached the bridge, captured and held it.

An hour later what remained of the Parachute Brigade was withdrawn and taken back to Syracuse by lorry.

The operation against the Primosole Bridge was successful, but the margin between success and failure was very small. Less than one-fifth of the Brigade was dropped at the right place and at the right time. The remainder was scattered over a wide area for the reasons already given. To these must be added the loss of eleven aircraft shot down and the return to base, for one cause or another, of twenty-seven without dropping their parachutists.

Thus the numbers of those available to capture the objective and then to repel counter-attacks were very small. Yet despite all setbacks the bridge over the Simeto was captured, lost and recaptured before the enemy had had time to destroy it, the advance of Montgomery's army was thereby secured and the campaign in Sicily once again shortened. This was accomplished at the cost to the 1st Parachute Brigade of twelve officers and 283 other ranks, of whom more than one-third were killed or wounded.

CHAPTER 8

THE AIRBORNE IN ITALY

THE CAMPAIGN AGAINST Italy herself was now about to be launched. The Germans had made every effort to reinforce the Italian mainland, and soon reached the correct conclusion that the main attack by the British and American invaders would be made in the neighbourhood of Naples. To guard, however, against the possibility, amounting almost to a certainty, that the Allies would create a diversion by landing in the extreme south, the Germans constituted a defence in Apulia and sent thither parachute troops weak in numbers but strong in resolution. Though they had serious misgivings, soon to be fully justified, regarding the staunchness of their ally, they could do no more. At the end of August, the Italians opened negotiations, of which the object was to secure an Armistice. Terms were agreed, and the date of its announcement was September 8th, twenty-four hours before the attack on the Italian mainland was delivered.

Four days before, Major-General Hopkinson, commanding the 1st Airborne Division, was ordered to occupy Taranto and hold it against all attack until the arrival of reinforcements. Aircraft to transport the airborne troops were not available, and it was therefore decided to put them ashore from a minelayer and live cruisers of the Royal Navy and one of the United States Navy. The division was to move in two parts. The first sailed at five o'clock on the afternoon of September 8th, after spending seven hours in strenuous, if somewhat confused, efforts to load their stores and equipment. Here the Royal Navy displayed that capacity to deal with the unexpected for which it has so justly a reputation. The decks of the cruisers were "cluttered up with the most heterogeneous collection of vehicles, stores and equipment," and a far higher number of officers and men were embarked than the orders, framed with official prudence, had dictated.

The main disappointment was the failure of H.M.S. Abdiel, the minelayer, to open her hatches wide enough to allow the entry of jeeps. They were six inches too narrow. She was able, however, to accommodate twelve six-pounder anti-tank guns.

On the arrival of the Force at the minefield covering the entrance to Taranto, the destroyer H.M.S. Javelin went in alone and returned two hours later with an Italian pilot on board. This time of waiting was enlivened by the spectacle of two Italian battleships of the Cavour class and many other warships "down on the horizon, stealing away to Malta, to give themselves up." At 5 p.m. precisely, twenty-four hours after the Squadron had sailed, H.M.S. Penelope, with the American cruiser Boise, steamed straight into the harbour, went alongside and began to unload. The rest of the force lay off and discharged their cargo by lighters.

Pushing on from Toronto

The 1st Airborne Division was soon streaming ashore and meeting with no opposition, pushed forward to cover the northern approaches to the town. Before dark General Hopkinson had met the Italian Military Governor and accepted his surrender. Divisional Headquarters was set up in the Albergo Europa, abandoned by the Germans that morning and bearing evidence of their late presence "in the form of bottles, standing orders and extensive murals depicting the strength of the German Navy."

The Italians in the town were vociferous in welcome, but vague in information. It was clear, however, that there were no Germans in Taranto. At midnight a great misfortune occurred. H.M.S. Abdiel, moving in to berth, struck a mine and blew up with a loud explosion. Some 130 officers and men of the 6th Parachute Battalion were lost, together with all the six-pounder anti-tank guns and the reserve of ammunition. Among the killed was its Commanding Officer.

Having secured the approaches to the city, the 4th Brigade continued its advance, while the 2nd held the port. By the morning of the next day, the 9th Reconnaissance Squadron had reached the small town of Massafra, where they endured the first of many enthusiastic receptions at the hands of a false, fickle but essentially peace-loving populace. From here an attack was made on Mottola, the next town on the main road leading to the port of Bari on the east coast. It was carried out by the 156th Parachute Battalion, some of whom arrived in jeeps which were left in charge of the cook, and others on bicycles, while "C" Company drove up in civilian buses, on which the leader flew the Trans-Jordan flag bestowed on the battalion some time previously by the Emir Abdullah. After a short and not very effective resistance, the enemy withdrew, and one of the first officers to enter the town was the Divisional Commander, whose reception and that of his troops was afterwards described as being "rather like the end of a rugger match," with the addition of large gifts of flowers and fruit. That evening the enemy ambushed one of our patrols, and the Reconnaissance Squadron of the Division captured a German Staff car and its occupants. Such small incidents are typical of many which occurred in the subsequent fighting. There is little doubt that the Germans had over-estimated our strength and were, moreover, unpleasantly aware that the men moving against them wore the redoubtable red beret. Yet the Division consisted of no more than 6,668 men with but sixteen six-pounder guns as their only artillery.

"To lend tone to the operation"

The advance continued with varying degrees of opposition. At Cassa del Duca the Commanding Officer of the 156th

Parachute Battalion had break-fast with the local Duke, who had had a hasty tea the previous afternoon with the retiring German Commander. The Brigadier with the Defence Platoon was involved in a sharp action and the day closed unhappily with the loss of General Hopkinson, who, mortally wounded in the head, died twenty-four hours later at Taranto. His place was taken by Brigadier E. E. Down, commanding the 2nd Parachute Brigade. The Germans were employing the tactics of delay, and held on to any ridge or building which offered good, if temporary, cover. A large, bright red building on a ridge north of the village of San Basilio was one of their many defensive positions.

Launching an artillery attack on it was a difficult matter. "A 149 mm. howitzer, carelessly left lying about by the Italians " was, however, discovered and pressed into service. It was loaded, aimed and "much to everyone's surprise, when fully cocked and with practically no charge, a direct hit was scored. Fortunately for the Italian Public Works Department the shell failed to explode."

The threat of bombardment sufficed, and the Germans yielded to an infantry attack. During it, "a star pupil of a Middle East Close Quarter Battle School expert justified himself of his master by bringing down a German officer at twenty-five yards with his pistol." Three more Italian howitzers were secured, but they lacked a number of important parts and there were no Italians to serve them. They "were intended," commented the Brigadier Commander "to disguise the scarcity of our troops on the ground, to give a little support and to lend . . . tone to the operation. Their antics may well have caused a little dismay to the enemy's troops. They certainly gave pleasure to our own."

On the evening of September 12th the remainder of the Division had arrived at Taranto, carried by the Royal Navy ; thus reinforced, the Division pushed on and captured Castellaneta. By then, however, its position was far from satisfactory. It was pursuing an enemy provided with a far larger number of vehicles than it possessed ; it was more than twenty miles from its base, was very thin on the ground and, possessing very little artillery, was in no position to withstand a determined counter-attack. Nevertheless, its Commander was determined to maintain the initiative. All its patrols were instructed to be as offensive as possible, and an effort was made to shell the town of Gioia, the next important place on the road. The task was assigned to one of the Italian 149 mm. howitzers, but after the first round, "the retaining nut came adrift," and the piece fell off its carriage.

To seize Gioia was a matter of increasing importance, for its airfield could then be used as a base from which fighters and fighter-bombers could operate over the hard-pressed British troops battling in the Salerno Bridgehead.

The situation was further complicated by the necessity to maintain a firm hold at all costs on the port of Taranto. It seemed impossible to do both, when very fortunately the enemy provided the solution by vacating Gioia on the night of September 16th/17th. In forty-eight hours six Squadrons of the Royal Air Force were in action from that base. On September 19th, the 4th Parachute Brigade were relieved by the 1st Air Landing Brigade, and soon afterwards the enemy withdrew into the area of Foggia under pressure from the Canadians advancing from the south-west. Thus ended nine days of interesting, though not heavy, fighting. For once the casualties suffered were very light, the total for the 4th Parachute Brigade being eleven officers and ninety other ranks killed, wounded or missing.

The Germans were on the run

The possibility that the Germans might attempt to counter-attack in force with the object of recapturing Taranto was still one of the chief preoccupations of the British High Command. Accordingly from September 20th to 24th the 1st Airborne Division was employed in constructing a defence perimeter to supplement the Italian fortifications of the port. Such a task was distasteful to men whose appetite for close contact with the enemy had been whetted, not diminished, by a year of strenuous campaigning.

Moreover, the Germans were undoubtedly on the run. The parachute troops, who had not seen a parachute for weeks, were eager to pursue them. It was therefore with rejoicing that they learnt that part of them, including the Air Landing Brigade, the Reconnaissance Squadron and the Independent Parachute Company, would, together with elements of the 78th Division constitute "A" Force, of which the object was to keep in close and constant contact with the enemy.

This task they fulfilled as far as they were permitted by the Germans, whose Commander at that time was pursuing the tactics of the Duke of Plazatoro and leading " his regiment from behind " in a swift undeviating retreat. On September 22nd the Air Landing Brigade occupied Foggia, but thereafter progress was slow, owing to the extensive demolitions carried out by the retiring foe. Sometimes, as at Ripalta, his sappers were discovered at work, and then they suffered the consequences. Throughout those days the Reconnaissance Squadron was especially active, being always in the forefront of the advance. Indeed, during the whole of this period, the only airborne troops thoroughly unhappy were the glider-pilots who "were still doing guard duties at Taranto." By the end of September infantry in adequate numbers had become available on this Front, and the presence of the highly trained Airborne Division was no longer necessary. Before taking temporary leave of them, however, mention must be made of their Auxiliary Services.

Sappers, Signallers and Surgeons

The Royal Engineers were assiduous in the performance of their many humdrum but exacting duties. Less than 400 all told, they took a foremost part in unloading equipment and stores when the Division landed ; they then put the railway system into working or "coaxed and threatened" the local Italians to clear the obstruction. The removal of mines and booby traps became a daily task, of which the monotony in no way diminished the danger, and they ended "with an unerring sense of history," by finding a ford in the River Ofanto on the scene of the battlefield of Cannae.

The Divisional Signallers were equally active, and made the greatest possible use on all occasions of the civilian telephone lines, many of which were intact. In taking them over, they were assisted by one Signor Martinez, soon nick-named Alf, who spoke fluent English. He worked tirelessly with skill and accuracy, asking only that he be given "two square meals a day."

During the advance the Signallers were hampered by lack of equipment, especially switchboards. An officer, sent to Sicily to obtain one which could operate forty lines, was informed that an instrument capable of dealing with but half that number was alone available. This was better than nothing, and he returned with a loaded packing-case which, when opened, was found to contain a forty-line instrument after all. During their sojourn in Italy, the Signallers of the Division dealt with over 69,000 messages, excluding local telephone calls at base, and each dispatch rider averaged somewhat more than eighty miles a day.

The R.A.S.C. were handicapped at all times by the very small quantity of transport available. Such vehicles as there were on the spot were antique and in bad repair, but the artificers, by dint of ceaseless work, maintained the casualty figures at as low a level as twenty per cent. The R.A.M.C. suffered at the outset from the loss of the Abdiel, which had carried all their medical equipment. This was soon replaced, however, and eventually five hospitals were established which proved adequate to cope with casualties.

By November 1943 the 1st Airborne Division had seen much fighting, endured many hardships and firmly established its reputation. Less than a year later this reputation was to be enhanced by deeds which will share the highest place among those performed by the British Army during its long, eventful, glorious history. Before describing the attack on the small Dutch town of Arnhem and its bridge across the Lower Rhine, the exploits of the 6th Airborne Division, destined to win much glory and renown in Normandy, must be considered.

CHAPTER 9

D DAY: THE SIXTH AIRBORNE PREPARES

WHILE THE 1st Airborne Division was engaged in the campaigns of North Africa, Sicily and Italy, those in authority at home had been busy organising the expansion of airborne forces ; but when in May 1943 the 6th Airborne Division was formed, its training and expansion were again limited by the number of aircraft available. It was placed under the command of Major-General R. N. Gale, D.S.O., O.B.E., M.C. Major-General R. E. Urquhart, D.S.O., was the other Divisional General, having taken over command of the 1st Airborne Division from Major-General Down. Browning assumed command over all airborne forces, and subsequently established a Corps Headquarters. With them, as an indispensable part of the organisation, was No. 38 Wing of the Royal Air Force, but many of its aircraft and crews were still in Africa. It was not until the summer and autumn of 1943 that its whole activity could be employed in the training of troops destined to play a part of the highest significance in what was hoped and believed would be the opening of the war's final stage-the invasion of the Continent of Europe.

It is possible that development would have been hastened if the full number of enthusiastic and skilful officers had been there to continue their long association with airborne troops. Unfortunately for those troops, for England, and for the Allies, they had already laid down their lives.

Squadron-Leader Wilkinson, who with Group Captain Cooper was an expert in the art of glider towing, had met death over the inhospitable hills of Sicily, flying a Halifax with a Horsa on tow to the attack on the Ponte Grande. Four days later Major

Lander, commanding the 21st Independent Parachute Company, who was an expert in the difficult business of dropping in advance of the gliders and making flarepaths to assist their landing, had been killed in the expedition against the Primosole Bridge. Wing Commanders P. Day and W. S. Barton, D.S.O., D.F.C., closely connected with the work of No. 38 Wing, were also dead, and to these losses must be added the deaths, already recorded, of Rock, Norman and Hopkinson. When a new arm is being developed, it is usually those intimately associated with its beginnings who run the greatest risk and pay the highest penalty. So it was in the early days of Bight ; so it was again when airborne troops began to play their part in war. Fortunately, ready to take the places of the pioneers were men endowed with the same enthusiasm and very soon the same degree of skill.

Glider training went on slowly and steadily ; larger and larger formations presently took the air. By November, exercises in which as many as forty gliders took part were being successfully mounted, and the methods of marshalling larger formations and putting them on the right route for their objective were being worked out, and could now be tried on a reasonable scale. In these unceasing labours the 9th United States Troop Carrying Command, by then in the United Kingdom, played a considerable part, and their enthusiastic help made possible a policy of expansion on a more generous scale than had at first been hoped or contemplated.

In January 1944 Air Vice-Marshal L. N. Hollinghurst, C.B., C.B.E., D.F.C., a most experienced officer, was appointed to command all the squadrons of the Royal Air Force now formed into several groups, for to that size had No. 38 Wing expanded. Stirlings and a number of Halifaxes no longer needed by Bomber Command were diverted to airborne work, and the training of their crews in the use of special devices to enhance the accuracy of navigation was put in hand. Such progress was made that on April 24th, 1944, an entire airborne division, the 6th, was taken into the air by the united efforts of the Royal Air Force and the United States Troop Carrying Command. On that day and the two following, it carried out an exercise which, though those who took part in it did not know it at the time, was a dress rehearsal for the invasion of Normandy six weeks later.

Throughout this long period, the lessons learnt by all three Services in Africa and Sicily were being studied and applied. One thing soon became very clear. No successful invasion of Europe could take place without airborne forces able and ready to leap over Germany's vaunted west wall and thus bring its formidable defences to no account. Every invasion plan, therefore, made provision for the use of parachutists and glider-borne troops.

The dropping zones are chosen The chances that they would succeed seemed in the spring of 1944 to be high, certainly high enough to justify the risk of using them. To begin with, the country in which they would operate was inhabited by people friendly to them, from whom aid of one kind or another might reasonably be expected. Then, too, it was known-that the quality of the German troops and equipment in France was very mixed. Some of it was good, but much of it was not. Most important of all, air superiority and, very possibly air supremacy, would be ours. This dominion over the enemy in the air was the determining factor in planning airborne operations which, if successful, would greatly lighten the heavy task of those who must invade by sea.

It was as far back as August 1943 that the use of airborne troops in the Caen-Bayeux area of Normandy was being studied. At first the dropping of an airborne division immediately in front of the seaborne invaders was considered ; but it was soon realized that, if they were spread over a wide area, they would be unable, lightly armed as they were, to offer serious resistance to the enemy's armour should he choose to use it in any strength against them. When General Montgomery, fresh from the triumphs of the 8th Army in the Mediterranean, arrived to take command of the invasion forces under the direction of the Supreme Commander, it did not take him long to decide that they would be best used in helping the 1st Corps to hold and protect the left flank of the British sector. How they were to do so will shortly become apparent.

Planning proceeded in detail through the late winter of 1943 and the spring of 1944. As information concerning conditions in Normandy flowed in, it became obvious that many of the landing zones tentatively chosen for gliders would not be suitable, for, as the reconnaissance photographs showed, the enemy was engaged in the erection of stout poles designed to over-set gliders at the moment of touching down. Consequently, wherever possible, parachute troops were substituted for glider borne, the first to be reinforced by the second when daylight revealed the best places where gliders could land with a reasonable chance of survival.

An unobtrusive house on Salisbury Plain

Many of the plans had been devised by a staff of Army and Air Force officers working in an unobtrusive house hiding among trees on Salisbury Plain. The precautions to maintain secrecy were elaborate and effective-almost too much so. There was but a single key to the house and, when one day the officer who possessed it was delayed, he found on arrival a throng of eager planners, most of them of field rank, in a state of high indignation, for the door was fast locked and entry by any other means was impossible, since all the windows were barred. For an hour the planners had had "to flee the time carelessly" in silence or in talk on more trivial matters, the nature of their occupation making it impossible for them to discuss what was uppermost in their minds outside in the churchyard which, absit omen, stood next to the house.

During the last weeks before the day of the invasion, the

volume of training increased. Of its exact and meticulous nature a striking example, the capture of the battery at Merville, will be given in a moment. It was during this period that Major-General Gale issued to his officers a general instruction on the conduct of the coming battle, in which he summed up the whole duty of the airborne soldier. "You must," he said, "possess tactical ability, you must take care of your men, and you must have a sound and properly working system of supply and maintenance of equipment."

The first duty of every commander, whatever his station, was to know what was expected of him. "It is not a question of what he wants to do but what he is wanted to do."

The degree of freedom allowed to subordinates in the method of carrying out their task was next emphasised. "You must remember," urged the General, "that it is your plan, and it must be your duty to ensure that it is your plan which is being carried out. Your responsibility in this is not one that you can be permitted to shirk. Your natural tendency may be to fight shy of it. You cannot ; for ultimately the edifice is yours, and its foundation and cornerstones must be laid by you." Gale then laid down, or rather reiterated, the principles on which an assault upon an enemy must always be based, and was especially emphatic on the manner in which the inevitable counter-attack must be met and defeated. "At night hold your fire," he advised, "and beat your enemy by guile. By day or by night you must lay traps for him. Laugh quietly at him if he falls into your snares, and when you have him, kick him in the pants." How best to do so was contained in a number of suggestions or maxims, and the General ended with a pregnant phrase. "What you get by stealth and guts," he said, "you must hold with skill and determination."

Waiting for the right weather

As May gave place to June the main anxiety of the airborne commanders - one which they shared with their naval and military colleagues - was the weather. Its importance to any enterprise of great pitch and moment needs no emphasis ; but the fact that the invaders of Normandy were to be taken to their destination in aircraft as well as in ships made suitable weather even more essential. When the revised plans for the raid on Dieppe, carried out not quite two years before, were being drafted, it had been found that weather favourable to the Navy might be unfavourable to the airborne troops. For that reason Commandos, not parachute battalions, had attacked the two main coastal batteries guarding the port. The attack on Dieppe was only a raid and, as always so rn such an operation, the hardest problem was not how to put the troops ashore but how to take them off again. What Ramsay Montgomery and Leigh Mallory were planning to carry out under Eisenhower was not a raid but an invasion. Provided, therefore, that the what weather conditions suitable for the airborne part of the task were not too unfavourable fo he Navy, the operation could be launched with a reasonable prospect of success. Meteorological experts, whose task no man envied, gave it as their opinion that, with due regard to the state ot the tide - a vital factor where the Navy was concerned - two days, the 5th and 6th of June, would be suitable. If the invasion did not take place on one of them, it would have to be postponed for at least a fortnight, so that the tide might once more be of the height and speed required.

All was ready for June 5th, but the forecast on the 4th was unfavourable, and the order to start could not be given. The further outlook was unsettled - so much so that the chief German meteorological officer gave it as hrs professional opinion that no invasion could take place on that day or the next. The Allied experts were of another view. Conditions on the night of June 5th/6th and for twenty four hours later, though not very good, would be possible. For General Eisenhower that was enough. In the slowly gathering dusk Air Chief Marshal Sir Trafford Leigh-Mallory, commanding the Allied Expeditionary Air Force, new from airfield to airfield to speak to the pilots and crews and take leave of troops, many of whom were to go into action for the first time.

Their equipment, if not perfect, had been devised and constructed in the light of experience gained by their predecessors at the risk and loss of many lives on the stony fields of Africa, the dusty olive yards of Sicily. The aircraft and the gliders in which they flew, though not so numerous as they might have hoped and expected after more than four years of war-there were not enough to carry the whole Division in one lift-were manned by well-trained and for the most part experienced crews. The officers and men themselves were most resolute and determined ; upon their right flank American Allies as well, if not better, equipped, and twice as numerous, were also to go into battle and to share with them the peril and the glory.

CHAPTER 10

JUMPING OVER THE WEST WALL

SUNSET HAD FADED from the sky when Air Vice-Marshal Hollinghurst took off in the first aircraft carrying the pathfinders. The invasion of Europe had begun and the airborne troops were in its van. The first men of them to land were Captains Tate and Midwood and Lieutenant de Lautour. They touched French soil between ten and twenty minutes past midnight, the foremost of the 22nd Independent Parachute Company. Their task, which they duly, if with some difficulty, accomplished, was to mark with lights the landing and dropping zones.

The 3rd and 5th Parachute Brigades, comprising the parachute element of the 6th Airborne Division, landed together and fought side by side. How they did so is best described by recounting the exploits of each brigade in turn. It was the duty of the 5th Parachute Brigade, under the command of Brigadier J. H. N. Poett, to land in the area north of Ranville and there to accomplish three tasks. They were first to seize the crossings over the river Orne and the Caen Canal near the villages of Benouville and Ranville. For this purpose six gliders carrying a special coup de main party were to be used. They were also to secure and hold the area surrounding these two villages and the village of Le Bas Ranville. Finally they were to clear and protect landing zones near Ranville and Benouville on which the gliders carrying the rest of the Division, on the evening of the first day, would touch down.

The part of Normandy in which these operations were to be carried out consists of high ground interspersed with valleys through which flow the rivers Orne and Dives. Separating them is a belt of ground well provided with woods, of which the largest is the Bois de Bavent. The pasture in the valleys is lush, and the rivers are bordered by reeds and thick, long grass.

There are a considerable number of open spaces in the form of fields devoted to pasture or tillage. The country depicted in the landscapes of Sisley and Monet, though belonging to a different part of France, closely resembles that in which the parachute and glider borne troops were to land.

The first and all-important task, the seizure of the two bridges, was to be accomplished by a force of six platoons of the 2nd Battalion of the Oxfordshire and Buckinghamshire Light Infantry, helped by a detachment of the Royal Engineers. Three of them were ordered to land within fifty yards of the east end of the swing bridge across the Caen Canal, and three within the same distance of the western end of the bridge across the River Orne. The bridges were to be seized immediately, and half an hour later the attackers would be reinforced by the 7th Parachute Battalion, who were to land near Ranville, 1,000 yards from the bridge over the Orne, To make certain that the parachute troops dropped in the right place, it was decided that pathfinders should land a short time before them, and set out navigational and other aids for the use of the parachutists.

Training for this very difficult and dangerous operation began in April, and Chatterton, in command of the Glider Pilot Regiment, was fortunate enough to discover a part of England bounded roughly by the four villages of Aston, Bampton, Buckland and Hinton, which is very much like that part of Normandy where the two bridges were situated. "Some weeks before the show we did an exercise," reports Major R. J. Howard, D.S.O., who led the attack on the swing bridge over the Caen Canal, "during which we 'pranged' the bridges at Lechlade. This was a tremendous help, for the place was very like the part of Normandy we subsequently attacked."

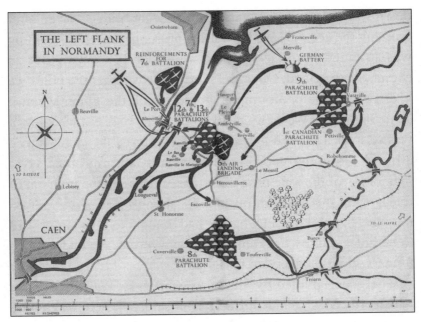

The left flank in Normandy

"We linked arms and braced ourselves"

Between 10.56 and 11.2 p.m. on the night of June 5th, six combinations of Halifaxes and Horsa gliders took off and presently reached a height of between 4,000 and 5,000 feet. Here patchy cloud was encountered, but otherwise weather conditions were good. June 6th was nine minutes old when the first combination crossed the French coast, soon followed by four others, the height then having increased to between 5,000 and 6,000 feet.

The sixth combination lost the way and made landfall about nine miles east of the River Dives. The gliders were all released the moment the coast was crossed, for it was necessary to cast off some distance away in order to make certain they would arrive at the bridges alone and unheralded, like thieves in the night.

The three destined to land near the bridge over the Caen Canal did so with complete success, glider No. P.F.800 touching down within forty-seven yards of the swing bridge. "Even after crossing the coast," says Howard, a passenger in it, "everything was so quiet that it seemed we were merely carrying out an exercise in England. Our chief worry was whether the poles we had seen on the photographs would wreck the glider when it came in to land. We were .ready to face this risk, but we knew it was serious. To guard against it as far as possible we all linked arms in the glider and braced ourselves, and my most vivid memory is of the long time that elapsed between the moment of release and the moment of landing, though it was only seven minutes. In point of fact what we had thought to be poles proved to be holes dug by the Hun a few days before. He had not had time to set up the wooden uprights."

The glider, piloted by Staff Sergeants J. H. Wallwork and J. Ainsworth, M.M., landed heavily, but safely. "There was a loud crash as the wheels came off, and sparks flashed past us. We thought we had 'bought' it because they looked like tracer bullets. In fact they were caused by the glider striking a wire fence. We had thrust up the exit door during the glide, and as soon as we came to rest I dived out and landed on my head. On getting to my feet my first impulse was to feel my limbs to see that they were all there."

The two other gliders landed close behind, and the troops in all three made haste to rush the bridge. Fire was opened upon them immediately, and Lieutenant Brotheridge fell mortally wounded, but the bridge was taken. Within a quarter of an hour, and while some dealt with the Germans in slit trenches nearby, the remainder made a defensive perimeter. Such of the German garrison as fought, N.C.Os. for the most part, did so bravely, but the men of whom they were in charge ran off into the night towards the sea. Their choice of direction was unfortunate, for they soon met with our newly landed seaborne forces and were destroyed.

The glider pilots were ordered to unload the heavy weapons

and to do so as quickly as possible, for the enemy were expected to counter-attack from Benouville at any moment. "That's a funny sort of make-up. You look like a Red Indian," said Howard to Sergeant Wallwork, the first pilot of his glider. "Then I realized it was his blood, for he had been badly cut by splinters of perspex and wood." The sergeant went on unloading the glider and then took his place in the defence. A Piat was rushed forward to cover the approaches to the bridge and placed in position near the café where Monsieur Gondrée and his wife had by that time realized that they were witnessing the invasion of Europe. It opened fire and destroyed the first of three old French tanks sent in by the Germans as the vanguard of their expected counter-attack. The tank was set on tire and its ammunition continued to explode for more than an hour, so that men of the 7th Parachute Battalion now on the way to reinforce, were under the impression that a great battle was raging at the bridge.

"Ham and jam" said a voice

While the Canal bridge was thus falling into British hands, that across the River Orne, a few hundred yards to the east, was also being attacked.

Here, too, success was immediate, one glider landing very close and the others 400 yards or so away. The attackers, under Lieutenant D. B. Fox, closely followed by Lieutenant T. J. Sweeney, M.C. and his platoon, seized the objective. Having crossed it, Sweeney found a small house on the other side in which "there was a little old lady and a little old man." In his best French he explained that he and his men had arrived "pour la libération de la France." The old couple were frightened ; they thought at first that he was a German carrying out an exercise for the purpose of deceiving the French inhabitants, who might thus be induced to give themselves away and provide new victims for the Gestapo. Such German ruses as this were greatly feared throughout the invasion area and go far to explain the

125

apparent indifference or covert hostility with which some of our troops were at first greeted. When dawn came, and with it light on the situation, the little old lady, realising what had happened, kissed Lieutenant Sweeney and made ready to rejoice. He, like Major Howard at the bridge over the canal, had been busy consolidating his bridge over the river. The sappers with both parties soon discovered that neither bridge had been prepared for demolition.

After a brush with a German patrol, the sound of grinding gears in the darkness seemed to betoken the presence of a tank, which, however, proved to be a German staff car with a motor cyclist behind it. The first burst of fire checked but did not stop the car and it roared over the bridge, only to be met with another and more accurate burst which sent it reeling into the ditch. Out of it was taken the German officer in command of the bridge defences, two empty wine bottles, a number of dirty plates, and a quantity of rouge and face-powder. Declaring that he had lost his honour by his failure to maintain the defences of the bridge, the officer asked for death. " I was a little worried," says Major Howard, "about the position on the bridge over the river, till I got on my wireless the code signal for victory. 'Ham and jam,' said a voice, 'ham and bloody jam.' Then I blew the V-sign on my whistle." Major Howard was reinforced by the arrival of Lieutenant Fox, fresh from his capture of the bridge at Ranville.

While these six platoons of the Oxfordshire and Buckinghamshire Light Infantry were thus engaged in securing the two bridges, those who were to reinforce them, the 7th Light Infantry Battalion of the Parachute Regiment, arrived in the area. A wind stronger than had been expected was blowing ; the battalion fell some distance from their chosen dropping zone and a number were killed in the air on the way down. On the orders of the commanding officer, Lieutenant-Colonel Pine-Coffin, D.S.O., M.C., who had landed with a bugler near the northern boundary, the regimental call was sounded at intervals. Its notes, piercing through the night, rallied many of the battalion, and by three o'clock in the morning it had reached the canal bridge and established a defence perimeter, "A" Company being in Benouville, "B" on a wooded escarpment farther inland, and "C" in the grounds of the local chateau. The situation was difficult and the immediate future uncertain, for Pine-Coffin had not more than 200 men with whom to protect the bridge.

Holding on to the bridgeheads

They were required to hold on and they did so, with ever-increasing difficulty but with an unfaltering spirit, until the main army had got ashore and could come to their relief. "A" Company was cut off in Benouville, where it held out for seventeen hours, losing all its officers killed or wounded.

During one of the numerous counter-attacks the enemy penetrated as far as the village and reached the Regimental Aid Post. Soon afterwards they were driven back, and in the confused fighting the well-beloved chaplain of the battalion, George Parry, lost his life. "B" Company, in the little hamlet of Le Port, passed an equally strenuous day. The place abounded in snipers, who fired from the top of the church tower till it was blown off by a shot from the Piat served by Corporal Killeen. A counter-attack from Caen with tanks was beaten off largely by the efforts of Private McGee, who destroyed a tank with a gammon bomb, and in so doing won the D.C.M.

On the canal itself, two gunboats, one coming from Ouistreham, the other from Caen, were dealt with. A fierce fight developed in the chateau grounds held by "C" Company, and a number of German Mark IV tanks were hit and set on tire. Between lulls the officer in command, Lieutenant Atkinson, conversed with the matron in charge of a number of civilian patients convalescing in the chateau. She was wearing trousers, seemed tired, but gave him all the information about the Germans that she possessed or could discover, and then went back to bed. One or two snipers wearing civilian clothes were found, notably a man in a morning coat and grey flannel trousers. They were killed or captured. Towards evening the pressure on the battalion had become very difficult to withstand. It was then that the hard-pressed men, lifting their heads, beheld the gliders coming in with the remainder of the Division and some much-needed stores. Their hearts were greatly lightened at this sight, "which," said Private Owen, "was the happiest I ever saw."

Certain moments are vivid in the minds of those who fought by the canal and the river from before dawn till after dusk on that long summer day.

There was the sound of Major Howard's victory signal travelling over the night wind to the ears of the parachutists struggling to reach and reinforce the bridge. There was the large hole which gaped in the side of the water tower at Benouville, hiding a nest of snipers. It had been punched by the first shot fired by a captured German anti-tank gun. There was Monsieur Gondrée in the little café by the swing bridge, tending the wounded and adding to the noise of battle a more convivial sound. He uncorked ninety-seven bottles of champagne, carefully hidden for just such a day as that: (the German occupying troops had been kept happy with a concoction made by his wife of rotting melons and half-fermented sugar, which they bought at twenty-five francs the glass and drank with avidity). There was Corporal Killeen reverently removing his steel helmet at the door of the church of which he had just smashed the sniper-infested tower. There were the red berets of General Gale and Brigadier Poett as they walked across the bridges about ten in the morning, "for all the world like umpires at an exercise".

There were the gliders "swaying and rustling" through the evening air, bringing reinforcements and supplies. And, above all, there was that moment when the straining ears of the airborne troops on and about the bridge heard at first afar off and then steadily nearer and nearer the shrill voice of bagpipes announcing the arrival of the 1st Special Service Brigade.

They had come in from the sea and fought their way inland, seeking to fulfil their promise that they would be at the Canal bridge by noon. When the skirl of the pipes could be no longer doubted, the temptation to reply by a bugle call in accordance with the prearranged plan was very strong. To do so would mean that the way was clear ; but it was not. The little hamlet of Le Port still harboured German snipers. Since they heard no bugle notes, the Commandos, on nearing Le Port, went into action. They helped to clear Le Port, and at two o'clock were heading for the bridge. On they came, Brigadier the Lord Lovat, D.S.O., M.C., at their head, with his piper behind him playing a shrill tune, and behind the piper the Commando soldiers marching in step. They reached the bridge and the green berets mingled with the red. Men of formations which had sustained the valour of British arms in the cold, clear fjords of Norway, in the dank jungles of Madagascar, in the stinging sands and stony hills of Africa, in the streets of Vasterival, in the tracer-lit docks of St. Nazaire, met with men who were performing for the first time a like office in the green fields of Normandy.

Establishing a perimeter while the bridges across the Caen Canal and the Orne were thus being successfully secured and held, the remainder of the 5th Parachute Brigade group were about their other tasks. The 12th and 13th Parachute Battalions had been detailed to seize the village of Le Bas de Ranville and the Ranville-le-Mariquet areas. To do so would be to establish a firm base east of the river and the canal, and- thus provide a starting point for subsequent operations. The 12th Battalion dropped at about 1 a.m. on June 6th and were widely scattered, for the wind was still high. Soon after landing, small parties of men began to dribble into the rendezvous, a quarry near the dropping zone. By 11 a.m. the battalion was taking up a line of defence round the village of Le Bas de Ranville, which was in their hands by 4 p.m. An hour later the Germans launched a heavy counter-attack supported by tanks, armoured fighting vehicles and self-propelled guns. A hedge on the right of the battalion's position was held by Lieutenant J. Sims, M.C., and twelve men, who allowed the Germans to come very close. Resisting the temptation to open fire on the clanking enemy guns, they engaged instead the infantry behind them, killed some twenty of them and then, having lost all but four of their number, withdrew a short distance, after holding the position for a very important hour and a half during which the rest of the defence was organised. Elsewhere, along the perimeter, after close and determined fighting, during which an enemy tank was destroyed by a gammon bomb, the Germans were beaten back.

For the rest of the day all was quiet, and that evening the 1st Battalion of the Royal Ulster Rides, which had landed from gliders with the rest of the Division, occupied Longueval. In the next day's fighting Private Hall of "A" Company of the 12th Parachute Battalion particularly distinguished himself. Eight German Mark IV tanks were leading the attack from the south, and one of the six-pounder anti-tank guns brought in by glider the evening before was standing silent, its crew dead around it. Hall loaded the gun, aimed it and knocked out two leading enemy tanks, firing but one round at each of then: He was about to dispose of the third when it received a mortar shell and blew up. The attack was repulsed, and that evening the 12th Battalion of the Devonshire Regiment arrived by sea and took over the position.

During those two days, especially on the first of them, the 13th Parachute Battalion was heavily engaged, mostly by the 125th Panzer Grenadier Regiment, whose attacks were repulsed after fierce fighting in which for a time the position was very critical, since the Germans succeeded in forcing their way momentarily into Ranville ; but at this juncture the hard-pressed parachute troops who, it should be remembered, because they had been scattered when dropped, had never been able to collect more than sixty per cent. of their available strength, were reinforced by No. 1 Commando.

The position was then held successfully.

Model for assault and battery

So much for the exploits of the 5th Parachute Brigade. Those of the 3rd, under Brigadier J. S. Hill, D.S.O., M.C., include one which must take its place among the finest actions ever undertaken against a specific objective.

The 3rd Brigade, like the 5th, had three main tasks. It was their duty to capture and destroy an enemy battery at Merville almost on the coast, of which the guns were sighted to take in flank the beaches on which the 3rd British Infantry Division, part of the great invading force, were to land.

They were also to demolish the bridges at Troarn, Bures, Robehomme and Varaville over the River Dives and the numerous waterways connected with it. Finally, they were to deny to the enemy the use of any roads leading into the area from the south and east. Much of their task was in the nature of a roving commission, and in fulfilling it they were performing one of the main duties of airborne troops, which is to harass the enemy, disrupt his communications, and create a condition of alarm and despondency in the areas immediately behind his forward troops.

Of these tasks, none was more important than that of destroying the battery at Map Reference 15576 near the little village of Merville. The battery in question consisted, it was thought, of four 150 mm. guns established in concrete emplacements twelve feet high and five feet deep, the thickness of the concrete walls being six feet six inches, and the roof above them covered with thirteen feet of earth. All doors which gave access to the position were made of steel, and the main armament was defended by one twenty mm. dual-purpose gun which could be used to combat attack from the air or land, and several machine-guns the exact number was uncertain.

The position was surrounded by a cattle fence which enclosed a minefield 100 yards in depth. This was bordered on its inner side by a barbed wire fence fifteen feet thick and five feet high, and in many places this fence had been doubled. At the seaward side of the battery was an anti-tank ditch fifteen feet wide and ten feet deep. To complete the defences, additional minefields had been laid across all the open approaches to the battery, and machine-guns had been sighted to cover them. It will be generally agreed that these defences were in the last degree formidable. They were held by between 180 and 200 men.

This, then, was the nut which had to be cracked, and the nutcrackers consisted of the 9th Battalion of the Parachute Regiment and three gliders manned by volunteers, whose stern duty it would be to land not near but on the battery. This was only possible if the pilots were prepared to crash-land their gliders and to rely on the concrete defences of the battery to tear off their wings, thus arresting the progress of the fuselages, which would contain three officers and forty-seven other ranks of the Battalion, and one officer and seven other ranks of the Royal Engineers.

To Lieutenant-Colonel T. B. H. Otway of the Royal Ulster Rifles was entrusted the formidable duty of silencing this battery, and he took over his command on April 2nd, His planning and preparations provide the promised example of how meticulously the preliminary measures are carried out before an airborne assault is delivered. After considering the problem for a week, he asked for and was given carte blanche in the matter of the rehearsals and other preparations indispensable for success. He chose a spot in England near Newbury, where conditions very similar to those which, would be met with in Normandy prevailed. The land was under cultivation and the crops on it valued at several thousand pounds ; but the necessities of war were paramount. Otway asked for the use of it on a Wednesday, and the Sappers began work upon it on the following Friday, permission to do so having been obtained in the meantime from seven different Ministries in Whitehall.

A complete and accurate reproduction of the battery 400 yards by 400 yards was constructed in a week, its shape and dimensions being determined from the numerous air photographs available. Tubular scaffolding was used to simulate the guns. In order to reproduce the exact conditions it was necessary not only to build the model to scale but also to level the ground covering the approaches to it. Four mechanical excavators and six large bulldozers, brought to the area by tank transporters from cities as far away as Liverpool and Plymouth, worked night and day, the hours of darkness being illumined by headlights. The maintenance of secrecy was of vital importance. To secure it, all roads leading to the area were closed and no one without a pass signed by the Commanding Officer himself could make use of them.

Most of the local landed gentry accepted these restrictions cheerfully, but a number, eager to maintain the rights of property, had to be pacified by drinks in the Mess. To make sure that every officer and man was maintaining his pledge of secrecy a number of specially trained and attractive young Women were sent into the area with orders to do their utmost to extract information from the troops. Their failure was complete. Nothing was revealed, although the whole plan had been deliberately divulged by Brigadier Hill to every officer and man, the only information withheld being the actual time and place of the attack. Thirty-five officers and 600 other ranks were continuously practised over a number of weeks till everyone knew his own precise duty and how to carry it out. Five rehearsals by day and four by night, all conducted with live ammunition, sufficed to give the troops an exact idea of what it was they were to accomplish.

On May 31st, after the battalion had moved from this training

133

area to the airfields from which they would take off, the special briefing for the operation was begun. It lasted five days, and every man attending it was required to submit to his immediate superior his own sketch, drawn from memory, of the part he had to play. The troops to be carried in the gliders had been chosen from volunteers called for from the battalion-no easy task, for not one man but demanded to be set in the post of utmost danger.

Let it be remarked in passing that not only would the gliders have to crash land on the battery, but they would have to do so under heavy fire from the assaulting Parachute Battalion.

On the morning of June 5th a drumhead service was conducted by the Reverend Gwinett, at which a special flag made by the Women's Voluntary Service of Oxford was dedicated, and before the take-off that evening, the Commanding Officer spoke personally to every officer and man in the battalion.

The plan-provided for two special parties to be dropped in advance, one to organise the rendezvous, the other to reconnoitre the battery. A third under the Second-in-Command was to create a firm base, while other parties were detailed to snipe the defenders of the battery and to create a diversion against any German troops in the immediate neighbourhood.

The main body of the battalion was to form the breaching and assault formations. They were to be provided with special equipment, carried in five gliders and including anti-tank guns, jeeps loaded with ammunition, and scaling ladders with which to cross the anti-tank ditch. Three gaps were to be blown in the battery defences by demolition parties, and the rest of the battalion would then enter the battery and there join their glider borne comrades in the task of killing or capturing anyone they found. As the assault went in, a party was to create a diversion at the main gate and ten minutes before, a hundred Lancasters were to bomb the battery.

"The Commanding Officer decided to advance"

The take-off gave rise to no special incident. Crossing the coast of France, the battalion ran into a moderate concentration of anti-aircraft fire. This caused very little disorganisation, but the strength of the wind was a more serious matter. The Dakotas of No. 46 Group, carrying the airborne troops, dropped them over a very wide area, one stick falling several miles away, for some of the navigators had mistaken the River Dives for the River Orne which was the pin-point. By ten minutes to three in the morning only 150 out of 600 men had reached the rendezvous and were ready to begin the approach march to the objective. One of them was the Commanding Officer, who, with the rest of his stick, had been flung untimely out of his Dakota as it was taking evasive action to avoid the flak. Lieutenant-Colonel Otway found himself heading straight for the roof of what he knew to be the headquarters of a German battalion. So accurately and clearly had the maps and models been prepared that, though he had never been there before, he knew exactly where he was. Missing the headquarters house by a few feet, he landed in the garden with one other man, who picked up a brick and flung it through a window through which the Germans were firing at them with revolvers. Presumably mistaking it for a bomb the enemy fled. Otway then made his way to the rendezvous, leaving behind him, unknown to himself, his batman, who had fallen through the roof of the greenhouse, but who subsequently rejoined him.

Once arrived, he found the state of affairs far less favourable than he had hoped. To quote from his staccato official report: "By 0250 hours the battalion had grown to 150 strong with twenty lengths of Bangalore torpedo. Each company was approximately thirty strong. Enough signals to carry on - no three-inch mortars-one machine-gun - one half of one sniping party-no six-pounder guns - no jeeps or trailers or any glider stores - no sappers - no field ambulance, but six unit medical orderlies-no mine detectors - one company commander missing. The Commanding Officer decided to advance immediately."

The hearts of the more fortunate remained unshaken, even when, on moving forward, they were attacked by a herd of maddened cows rushing wildly across a field in the quiet moonlight. Fortunately the reconnaissance party had been dropped in the right place. They had been somewhat shaken by the bombing attack of the Lancasters, for it "had missed the battery completely," but the bombs had fallen very close to the reconnaissance party. By the time the advance began, this party had cut gaps in the outer cattle fence, penetrated the minefield, and lain down for half an hour beside the inner belt of wire, where they observed the enemy posts, discovering their exact whereabouts by listening to the conversation of the sentries.

They were presently joined by a party whose duty it was to lay white tapes to show the way. Only half of these men had been delivered at the right place and all the tapes were missing. The approaches were therefore marked "by digging heel marks in the dust." This vital preliminary work was accomplished without the loss of a single man, though those engaged on it were without mine detectors and had to neutralise the various trip wires by feeling for them with their hands.

Two gliders circling overhead

Meanwhile the much-depleted battalion, heavily shelled by guns firing on fixed lines, was advancing to the assault. On reaching the position chosen for the firm base, they came under the fire of six enemy machine-guns. The battalion's solitary machine-gunner was sent to do his best to quieten these.

He silenced the HTC of three of them. The other three were put out of action by the party moving against the main gate. As the battalion reached the outer defences two of the three gliders - the tow rope of the third had parted early and it had landed in

England to the chagrin of its occupants - appeared circling overhead. It had been decided to signal to them by firing flares from the mortars ; but there were no mortars, no flares, and consequently no signals.

The pilot of the leading glider, Staff Sergeant S. G. Bone, had had to overcome many difficulties on the way over. Weather conditions were unfavourable, with much cloud, which had to be avoided as far as possible by weaving. In mid-Channel the arrester parachute gear, a device designed to check the speed of a glider as it comes in to land, opened suddenly. This mishap caused the combination to stall and lose height. The gear was jettisoned immediately, but the tail unit of the Horsa had been badly strained. On reaching the French coast, flying beneath cloud which was 10/10ths at 1,000 feet, the combination came under anti-aircraft fire and was repeatedly hit.

Nevertheless, the Albemarle tug, with Pilot Officer Garnett at the controls, flew steadily on and circled what was believed to be the objective four times before releasing the glider. On the way down, Staff Sergeant Bone at first thought that the village of Merville was the battery, but at 500 feet he realized his mistake, turned away and landed eventually about half a mile from the objective.

The other glider, piloted by Staff Sergeant D. F. Kerr, had four casualties from flak when crossing the coast and, like its predecessor, was towed four times round the area before release. Coming in to land, Kerr saw that he would not quite be able to reach the battery. He therefore streamed his parachutes and crashed into an orchard only fifty yards from the perimeter.

Though he had failed to put his passengers into the very midst of the enemy in accordance with the plan, yet they were able to play a very important part in the fight ; for hardly had they left the glider when they encountered a German platoon hurrying to reinforce the garrison of the battery. Out-numbered more than two to one and dazed by the shock of their landing, the troops and the glider pilots nevertheless defended the orchard with the greatest vigour for four hours. Not a single man of the enemy got through to help the hard-pressed defenders of the battery.

Hard-pressed indeed, for Otway was pushing his assault regardless of the consequences. Two gaps were blown by the Bangalore torpedoes in the wire; then the attackers streamed in, and at once engaged in hand to hand fighting with the German gunners. These offered a stout resistance until one of them, seeing the badges of his opposite, screamed "Paratruppen," whereupon such as were left alive, twenty-two in number, surrendered. The guns, which were found to be seventy-five mm., were then destroyed by gammon bombs.

So at a cost of five officers and sixty-five other ranks killed or wounded, was accomplished a fine feat of arms whose success was of the greatest help to the seaborne invading forces. Among the victors was the battalion signals officer, who was seen by his Colonel to be fumbling in the blouse of his battledress. "What are you doing?" asked Otway. "Sending a signal home, sir," was the answer, and from his breast he withdrew a somewhat crumpled carrier pigeon, which arrived in England a few hours later with a message recording the success of the operation.

Having captured the battery, the battalion, now reduced to eighty of all ranks, moved on to carry out its second task, the seizure of some high ground near Le Plein. On approaching the village of Hauger, the Commanding Officer was warned by a Frenchman that some 200 of the enemy were there entrenched ready to dispute his arrival. Almost immediately afterwards battle was joined. It was by now full daylight, and Otway could see that the main opposition offered by the enemies came from one particular house.

It was attacked by thirty men, but since it was loopholed for defence and surrounded by a wall six feet high, it proved too strong to be taken. In point of fact, the garrison of the village was composed for the most part of Russians forced to fight by the Germans, and informed that if they fell alive into the hands of the Allies they would be shot as traitors. This in all probability accounts for the strength of the resistance offered. The battalion was not strong enough to capture the feature immediately, and therefore went to ground and suffered much from snipers; but, when it had been reinforced the next afternoon by the 1st Special Service Brigade, the village was successfully cleared.

CHAPTER 11

THE LEFT FLANK HELD FIRM

THE REMAINING OPERATIONS of the Brigade can be but briefly recorded. The 1st Canadian Parachute Battalion, formed and trained during two years' hard work beginning in August 1942, dropped in the general area round the villages of Varaville and Robehomme on the River Dives. Their task was to destroy the bridges at those places, and, though they were widely scattered, they did so successfully without much opposition, and subsequently held a position not far from the Bois de Bavent.

The 8th Parachute Battalion, whose task it was to destroy the two bridges over the same river at Bures and the bridge at Troarn, had more difficulty.

Two and a half hours after the drop, its Commanding Officer, Lieutenant-Colonel R S Pearson D S O M C had only succeeded in collecting 120 all ranks. Among them were no Royal Engineers or machine gunners, and there were explosives enough to destroy only two of the three bridges. He moved first on those at Bures. In the meantime a detachment of Royal Engineers had landed on the northern outskirts of the Bois de Bavent. They collected a satisfactory quantity of explosive and demolition equipment from the kitbags and container loads dropped with them and moved off in two parties, one marching towards Bures, dragging their equipment with them on trolleys, the other making for the more distant Troarn in a jeep.

The first party soon fell in with the reconnaissance party of the 8th Parachute Battalion, who covered them while, according to plan, they destroyed the two bridges. The Sappers in the Jeep going to Troarn, Major J C A Roseveare and seven other ranks travelled at high speed, their Bren and Sten guns at the ready. At a level crossing near the town they ran into a barbed wire knife rest and it took them twenty minutes to cut themselves and then vehicle free. Though by that time the German garrison had been thoroughly aroused, the Sappers would not be turned from their task. Putting on full speed, they rushed through the town firing then Sten guns, Sapper Peachey acting as a rear gunner and making excellent practice. Immediately beyond Troan the road falls steeply. Down the hill sped the jeep under a hail of machine gun bullets, all of them fortunately flicking just above the heads of its occupants. The bridge was reached, and five minutes later a gap twenty feet wide had been blown in it. The Jeep was then ditched and the party moved on foot to a rendezvous at Le Mesnil.

Throughout the day many other Sappers arrived at that place, having had a number of brisk encounters with the enemy. Some had landed close to Ranville and been made prisoner for a time. But not for long : one of them Sergeant Jones, snatched a Schmeisser from a German and with it killed eight of his captors. Another Sapper Thomas, though wounded while still in the air, on landing wiped out with grenades a party of three who had been shooting at him. One aircraft took such violent evasive action that the parachutists in it were thrown flat and fell out one by one, at intervals, the stick stretching from Varaville to Robehomme, a distance of two miles. At both these places the bridges were successfully destroyed. In the British Army the Royal Engineers enjoy a reputation for courageous eccentricity. It was enhanced that day by Captain A. J. Jack, who, having blown the bridge at Robehomme, sat down with his men, cooked and ate breakfast, heedless of the warnings volunteered by the local inhabitants that the enemy might appear at any moment. Such coolness did much to inspire the French and increase the already high lighting qualities of his men.

While these Sappers were blowing the bridges, others had

dropped on the landing zone chosen for the gliders in which the Brigade and Divisional Headquarters, together with a certain quantity of anti-tank guns, were being carried. The fields forming the zone had been partially obstructed by poles.

These the Sappers soon removed and then set about laying out the landing strips. The lights upon them proved difficult to see, and when the gliders came in "some passed each other within thirty feet, going in opposite directions, but with the traditional ability of the Horsa to take punishment, casualties were very few." The two airborne bulldozers carried were particularly useful. One of them broke through the floor of its glider but safely survived the subsequent crash to the ground, and both machines were working on strips within an hour of landing. In eight hours, which was well within the margin of time allotted, they had cleared the four strips of glider debris, and filled in the holes which had been dug by the enemy to receive poles. Their operators worked without pause or intermission, all the time under sniper, mortar and shell tire.

The confused nature of that night's happenings is well illustrated by the adventures of an anonymous captain, the first to jump from his aircraft. He landed alone in the middle of the River Dives, climbed out and reached a farm, where he picked up four parachute soldiers. A young French boy undertook to lead them to their destination, Varaville, which they reached about 3.30 in the morning. "Complete chaos seemed to reign in the village. Against a background of Brens, Spandaus and grenades could be heard the shouts of British and Canadians, Germans and Russians. There was obviously a battle in progress." The captain and his party determined to make for Le Mesnil, where he knew the Brigade was to establish a firm base. An Englishwoman, a cockney from Camberwell, about fifty-five years old, then made her appearance and explained what was wanted to their young French guide. On the way to Le Mesnil they entered a wood and had a brush with a German patrol. One of the enemy threw a stick grenade which burst on the French boy's head and killed him. The party had now lost their guide, "their maps were not fit to use and they had already tramped for two miles through swamps with the water often chest high."

After a time they fell in with some French farmers who gave them fresh milk and bread. It was now light, and for all that day the party, swollen to about twenty, moved through the fields and through the Bois de Bavent.

By four o'clock in the afternoon, after they had crossed a number of canals twenty feet deep and "were all completely whacked," they saw the gliders carrying the rest of the Division coming in to land. "This exhilarating sight revived their spirits, which soared still higher when they saw some Spitfires . . . bring a couple of Messerschmitts down into the swamp quite close to them. They struggled on, not daring to rest in the swamp for fear of drowning." By ten in the evening they reached terra firma at last, having taken six hours to cover two miles through the swamp. They had still not reached Le Mesnil but were eventually put on the right road by "a very drunken Frenchman."

How the store-carrying gliders fared The plan for the store-carrying gliders was that they should land, some on each of the dropping zones, a short time before the arrival of the parachutists.

Like the gliders, which took part in the attack on the battery at Merville, all those ordered to land on the dropping zones experienced bad weather conditions, accentuated by the huge clouds of smoke and dust caused by bombing. About half the gliders detailed to land north of Petiville did so successfully, though their unloading took a long time. Those landing between Toufréville and Cuverville were less fortunate, only one-third reaching their destination, the remainder, save for one which was lost, landing on another dropping zone. The third group of gliders was to land between Ranville and Amfréville in the area nearest the vital bridges over the Orne and the Caen Canal, and close to the spot which had been chosen for Divisional Headquarters. Here a high measure of success was attained, for forty-nine out of the seventy-two gliders which took off landed according to plan. Five made forced landings in the United Kingdom, three in the sea, and fourteen were lost.

Once on the ground the glider pilots, fighting as a unit, were soon in action. By the evening ninety-three, composing "Force John," were well dug in and defending the zone from the south-west. One of them, Captain B. Murdoch, presently found himself involved in a brisk action against tanks.

He was acting as loader at the time to a six-pounder anti-tank gun, of which the layer was killed. Captain Murdoch took over, and he and the other gunners succeeded in destroying four out of five enemy tanks.

Of the fourteen gliders which failed to reach their destination, one, piloted by Major J. F. Lyne, was hit by flak in the tail when crossing the coast and the tow rope broke. The glider was in cloud and immediately began to descend. On coming out into clear air it was again hit, a shell bursting in the centre of the fuselage and damaging the jeep on board, but hurting no one.

Beneath was darkness shot with fire, and to choose a suitable spot on which to land was even more difficult than usual. The glider sailed remorselessly earthward, and at the last moment a pale patch, which "seemed to be a little less dark than the rest of the countryside," loomed up. It was an orchard, and into it Major Lyne crashed his glider, breaking his foot and cutting the face of his second pilot. These were the only mishaps.

The party of seven set off, their one object being to find someone who could tell them where they were. They soon ran into Germans, lay up in a field till dawn, and then found a farmer who directed them towards the River Dives. This they swam, and joined up with some Canadian parachute troops isolated near Robehomme. By then they were entirely surrounded by the enemy, and it took them three days to reach Ranville.

Throughout that time the French inhabitants were of the greatest help, and their grapevine information service enabled Lyne and his men to know at all times the exact position of the enemy. During their wanderings they met with a farm labourer and his family who produced as evidence of their love of England "a portrait of Queen Victoria tastefully executed in Nottingham lace," and provided them with a meal, a map torn from a school atlas, and two pocket dictionaries.

Eventually Major Lyne and the rest entered the Bois de Bavent, and there, though exhausted by forty-eight hours of stumbling through swampy ground, hiding in ditches, swimming streams and thrusting their way through unyielding undergrowth, reached at long last a road running in the right direction.

At that moment the enemy appeared. The weary men went at once into action with their personal weapons. "We managed to eliminate two lorry-loads of Germans and a car with four officers in it," reports Major Lyne, "by the simple process of throwing hand grenades at them. They were all wiped out. By this time we were all very tired." When they eventually reached the landing zone, after another fight, they had marched forty-five miles from the place where the glider had landed.

Men like these and their comrades, stubbornly holding the boundaries of the landing zones, made possible that mass landing of gliders on the evening of the first day which had been watched so thankfully by Private Owen from his slit trench on the bank of the Caen Canal. Every Hamilcar carrying the heavy stores, and 112 out of 114 Horsas, landed according .to plan, and from them poured the remainder of the Division, consisting of the 6th Air Landing Brigade and a number of other units including the Armoured Reconnaissance Regiment. The success of this operation is the best tribute to those who had first shown on the dusty fields of Sicily what skill and gallantry can achieve in the handling of a new and hazardous vehicle for the carriage of troops to battle.

The German counter-attacks begin

So by the end of the first two days the 6th Airborne Division was established firmly on the eastern bank of the River Orne, holding a half-circle round the little villages of Ranville, Le Mariquet and Herouvillette, with the 1st Special Service Brigade under their orders on the high ground of Le Plein and near the little village of Bréville, soon to become the scene of a fierce battle. The fighting during those forty-eight hours had gained for the Division all its objectives with the exception of a small coastal strip near Franceville. They had suffered 800 casualties, and more than 1,000 parachutists had not yet reached their rendezvous.

It was hoped and intended very soon to relieve them by troops coming in from the sea, but for various reasons this hope dwindled and then faded.

The days passed, and then the weeks and then the months, and still the Division fought on. It was a battle of defence against very heavy pressure from the best formations which Rommel and his successor, Von Kluge, could throw against them. To describe it in detail is not possible within the compass of a short account ; but one battle, the capture and retention of the village of Bréville, is of special importance, not merely as an illustration of the kind of warfare which the Division was called upon to wage in Normandy, but because defeat at that moment might have had the most serious consequences.

The days immediately following the landing were spent by the Division in consolidating its position, beating off counter-attacks, and welcoming the arrival of small, scattered bodies of parachute troops, who gradually made their way, marching like good soldiers, to the sound of the guns. Their adventures had been many. Here are two. A parachute soldier landed in the garden of an enemy headquarters in Herouvillette and, hearing a quiet call of "Tommy," flung a grenade in the direction of the voice, fortunately without effect, for the speaker was a member of the Forces Francaises de l'Intérieure and guided him to safety. Then there was the G.S.O.1 of the Division, who landed among mines at Varaville and fought all day with " a surprising number of snipers." During one of these engagements his steel helmet was struck so violently by a fragment of mortar bomb that the dent caused knocked it out of shape and made it impossible to wear, though the officer escaped with a scalp wound. Brigadier Poet's account of the actions of his brigade paints a picture of resolute and controlled fighting in which the battle swayed now to one side, now to the other, among villages of yellow-grey stone with the lovely names of Herouvillette, Longueval and St. Honorine.

"Distributed amongst the brigade positions we had some forty anti-tank guns. I was therefore praying for a German counter-attack, My prayers were answered on June 8th. Preceded by heavy concentrations from mortars and S.P. guns, the counter-attack developed from St. Honorine towards Le Bas de Ranville, but only in a disappointingly small way as regards the numbers of tanks that disclosed themselves. Only three Tiger tanks and one armoured car were actually located, but others were undoubtedly Bring from concealed positions. The counter-attack was decisively defeated, although some infiltration by infantry continued for a time."

The battle of Bréville

The Germans did not take very long to recover from the surprise of the airborne landings, and their counter-attacks soon developed in force.

For three days the battle raged in or near the small village of Breville, near the high ground of Le Plein which had been so desperately held against the assaults of the 9th Parachute Battalion on the morning of the invasion. There was no doubt that the enemy, who had succeeded in holding the village, was seeking to make a determined thrust from it towards the coast.

If successful, he would cut the Airborne Division in half and be in a position to threaten the left Hank of the whole British Army. A small gap had indeed already been made and very heavy casualties caused to the Special Service Brigade and the 12th Parachute Battalion. The enemy was determined to widen this gap if he could, and by the evening of the 10th he had almost succeeded. On the next day the 51st Division, with bitter memories of St. Valéry in their hearts, made a resolute attempt to drive tack the Germans and close the gap.

Their leading regiment, a battalion of the Black Watch, suffered very heavily and gained nothing by its resolution. Brigadier Hill, hastily mustering all the men he could, mostly tough Canadian parachute soldiers in action for the first time, led a counter-attack which temporarily restored the situation. The position, however, was very grave, almost desperate. Gale, the Divisional Commander, realized that the Brigade was in no position to withstand another attack. He realized also that the enemy was in bad shape and had lost at least as many men as the defence. The exhaustion on both sides was very great, but which was the more exhausted ? Gale believed that it was the enemy, and therefore determined, despite the very few troops at his disposal, to launch one more attack at the moment when the summer dusk deepened into night. His only reserve was the gallant 12th Parachute Battalion, now but 300 strong, and "B" Company of the 12th Battalion of the Devonshire Regiment. He had also a squadron of Sherman tanks, and all the available artillery in the neighbourhood, which comprised five field and one medium regiment.

The 12th Parachute Battalion, which had been resting all day, was ordered to make ready that evening. The men were concentrated in the church at Amfréville, where they waited until ten p.m. Then they left the church, formed up outside, and whiled away another five minutes reading copies of Pegasus, the

Divisional newspaper, handed out to them by the chaplain.

The order came to advance and they went forward, following a wall of smoke and flame and noise. Some of the houses in the village began to burn so brightly that dusk was turned into the semblance of a red dawn.

The fight was short but very fierce, for the airborne troops would be content with nothing but victory. "B" Company, rising from a field of clover, reached the edge of the village, killed a number of Germans in slit trenches and then went through between the burning houses to an orchard on the other side, where they dug in and held on. "C" Company attacked on the left and lost their reserve platoon by shellfire before they started. They reached a hedge held by the enemy and sought to use the bayonet, but the Germans would not stay for them and fled. The Devons were less fortunate.

They suffered very heavy casualties during the time spent in forming up for the attack, and only a few of them reached the village.

At one moment, soon after the loss of Lieutenant-Colonel A. P. Johnston, D.S.O., commanding the 12th Parachute Battalion, the position was critical.

It was saved by Colonel R. G. Parker, D.S.O., Deputy Commander of the 6th Air Landing Brigade who, although himself wounded in the hand, assumed command and set by his leadership an example which " was a big factor in the success " of the battalion. The enemy's guns were tackled and silenced by the Sherman tanks, and Within an hour the village was taken, and the gap closed. The news of victory was brought to Brigadiers Lord Lovat and the Hon. A. K. M. Kindersley, C.B.E., as they lay badly wounded in the aid post. That night the airborne troops ranged through the burning village dealing with snipers, one of whom was found lying dead in bed with, above his head, a notice written in English pinned to the wall with his knife, "Even if we fight alone, England must fall."

The 6th Airborne - In advance of the van

For the remainder of the month of June, for all July, and for the first fortnight of August, the Division held the line, suffering casualties, notably in the fighting round Le Mesnil, but each time giving much more than they received. Then at last, on August 17th, the order for a general advance came, and in ten days the airborne troops, now reinforced with some stout Dutch and Belgian regiments, swept forward up to the outskirts of Le Havre.

So rapid and pertinacious were they, that the enemy had no chance to stand and fight, despite the nature of the country, which is well wooded and cut up by streams and rivers, the chief being the Touges.` Gale gave them no rest, moving his brigades in a series of leapfrogs, and delivering his attacks both by day and night. The first main action was fought at Putot en Auge, which was captured during a night attack by the 7th, 12th and 13th Parachute Battalions on August 19th, when "the fighting spirit of the troops was beyond all praise." They had had no sleep for forty-eight hours, "yet throughout the day their dash and energy never diminished and in the evening they were in tremendous heart."

Next came the fight for Pont L'Evéque. Here the crossing of the river was " to be forced immediately at all costs," so as to leave the enemy no time to consolidate. The assault took place under cover of smoke and proved a hard tasks A few men got over the river near a ford and a larger number by means of a broken railway bridge. A troop of tanks was held up, but an armoured bulldozer succeeded in pushing sufficient débris from the burning houses of Pont L'Evéque into the stream, and the tanks were able to reach the other side. At one moment the gallant 13th Battalion had to withdraw from their small bridgehead, and despite every effort during two days and a night of hard fighting it proved impossible to eject the enemy. His casualties, however, had been so severe that on the night of August 23rd/24th he slipped away. There was finally the capture of Pont Audemer, which was accomplished on August 26th.

As mile after mile of this advance from the Orne and the Dives was covered and the sun of victory shone ever brighter and brighter, the men forgot their fatigue, forgot that they had been holding the line as ordinary infantry, and realized only that they were the victors. "I regard this march as definitely one of the outstanding feats of the battalion," writes a Commanding Officer.

"It was expected that men would fall out with foot trouble ; ambulances were, in fact, following up to lift such cases. The battalion, as stated, led the column and marched at light infantry pace, rapidly drawing farther and farther ahead. Not a single man fell out."

The leading elements of the Devons, who had reached Touges on August 24th, commandeered a Fire engine and a milk float, and in these set out for Honfleur. Being run on coal gas, neither vehicle could surmount the hills.

The first was driven by a fireman wearing a brass helmet, the second by its owner, the milkman ; they took the leading platoon, somewhat hampered by the presence of an interpreter whose knowledge of English was less than theirs of French, to within a mile and a half of the town. Thence the Devons went forward on foot, and presently found themselves in its main square surrounded by cheering men and women, of whom many were armed with rifles. These went off at frequent intervals until "we explained to them the use of the safety catch."

The enemy was still in the town and there was much sniping, but this did not deter the eager citizens from greeting with an almost embarrassing enthusiasm the Allies who had marched so far and accomplished so much.

"We had a warm welcome from the Mademoiselles," Rawson, "and a greengrocer opened his entire shop for us." The citizens rejoiced, and the sound of their cheering echoed all over Europe. There for a moment we can leave the gallant 6th Airborne. They had done more than win their spurs ; they had taken part in the most remarkable of all the invasions which the Continent of Europe has had to endure. It was an invasion not of savages thirsty for loot and women and conquest, but of liberators come to undo the deeds of savages whom to describe as Huns is to insult the followers of Attila. That must always be their pride and their reward.

CHAPTER 12

ARNHEM:
THE DOORSTEP OF GERMANY

BY AUGUST 17th, 1944, the German armies, which four years and three months previously, had overrun so swiftly the whole land of France, were retreating even more swiftly towards their own country. More than a million men, British and American, bursting from their congested bridgeheads in Normandy, were sweeping, in a fury of controlled vengeance towards Germany. The Americans were soon to reach the Vosges and to link with the army of General Patch moving up from the Mediterranean ; The British composing the 21st Army Group, presently crossed the Siene and the Somme and did not halt till they were well beyond Brussells. To this great victory the contribution of airborne troops was considerable. Apart from the 6th Airborne Division, far to the south, in the vanguard of General Patch's invading army, were other airborne troops, tough sons of America, some of whom went to battle in British gliders flown by British pilots. Thirty-eight Horsas took them from a dusty in Rome to a still dustier one on Corsica, and thence to their landing zone near the little town of Frèjus on the French Riviera.

While these battles were being fought the tired veterans of 1st Airborne Division, now at full strength again, were waiting on the Berkshire Downs and in the windy spaces of Salisbury Plain, with an impatience they took small pains to conceal, to play their part in what might ultimately prove to be the final discomfiture of the enemy. At one time the period of waiting seemed likely to be long, for between June 6th and September 17th no less than sixteen airborne operations to support the Allied Expeditionary

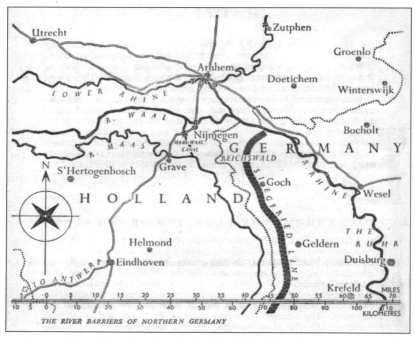

The river barriers of Northern Germany

Force were planned, and all of them came to naught. The reason was simple. Time is needed to plan an airborne attack – not very much time, but enough to ensure that the aircraft and the men to be carried in them are ready and are accurately briefed ; for – and it is impossible to emphasise this too often – no airborne attack can succeed unless each man taking part in it knows exactly what to do and when to do it. On each of those sixteen occasions, before the moment for take-off arrived, the armies in the field had either reached or were threatening the proposed objective or the delay imposed by the enemy made the success of an airborne operation impossible. Action, therefore, by airborne forces was not necessary. So these fine troops had perforce to remain in chafing idleness till they were called upon to resolve a situation created by an advance which had exceeded all expectations, especially those of the Germans.

By the middle of September the British 2nd Army had broken

154

through, crossed the Seine, advanced to Brussels and penetrated into Holland. To make this possible, the whole of its transport had been placed at the disposal of its leading Corps, and the other Corps had had perforce to remain more or less immobile. Even so, by the time the main body of the Corps had reached the Brussels-Antwerp line, the situation in regard to supply was already critical. That of the German forces opposed to them, however, was still more so. It may justly be described as chaotic. No organised resistance beyond the Seine had been possible, and it seemed that the remnants of the German 15th Army, which had been allotted the task of defending the Channel coast, were faced with but two alternatives. Either they could retreat into the fortified Channel ports of Boulogne, Calais, Dunkirk, and Ostend and there sustain themselves as long as possible, or they could try to find a way out into southern Belgium and Holland and, if successful, attempt to re-form behind the barriers which nature has there provided.

For a day or two something akin to panic seems to have prevailed among the German forces in the Dutch islands and on the mainland itself They had but one defensive position left before the Rhine and the frontiers of their country. It was provided by three rivers : the Meuse, which, when it crosses the Dutch frontier, becomes the Maas ; the Waal, which is the main branch of the German Rhine ; and the Lower Rhine. Had its difficulties of supply been overcome, there is little doubt that the 2nd Army might have pushed through and reached Germany. Yet this was impossible. The main lines of supply still ran from Cherbourg and the artificial port of Arromanches, and large stocks of all sorts were held in dumps near these ports ; but road and rail communications between this base area and the front, over 250 miles away, were not equal to the task of supplying large forces which were still on the move and making heavy demands on stores of every kind. Thus were the Germans given breathing space, and they used it to the utmost.

The river barriers of Germany

The line of the Albert Canal was defended by what was left of the 15th Army, by detachments of the Hitler Jugend sent with all speed from Germany, and by such garrison troops as were available on the spot. The panic was ruthlessly checked by the adoption of the sternest measures, and as the days slipped by and the British armies made no further movement, the Germans consolidated their defence. Its most important section was that covered by the line of the three rivers just mentioned. Behind them was but a skeleton, for the Siegfried Line here peters out in the neighbourhood of the Reichswald. Between the end of this forest and the Waal at Nijmegen runs a ridge of ground which, though it is only 633 feet at its highest point above sea-level, constitutes the only range of hills in Holland. It is heavily wooded, but from the top it is possible to observe the country for a long distance in every direction. For many years this ridge had formed the favourite exercise ground for the Dutch Army, and the canal connecting the Maas with the Waal, and the Maas itself, running respectively along the western and southern sides of this hill, made it an ideal defensive position.

The Germans were quick to reinforce its natural strength by every possible means. There is no doubt that they feared an attack by airborne troops, and during the first fortnight of September they made all possible preparations to meet it. More and more anti-aircraft guns were brought up, and reconnaissance photographs showed each day some new position where work on digging them in had begun. Agents reported that the Dutch population, including twelve-year-old children, were being pressed into service to prepare a main defence line running along the Waal to the sea and a forward line following the Maas.

Field-Marshal Montgomery had two courses open to him. Either he could remain where he was, content with an advance which, in less than a month, had brought him to the threshold of

Germany, or he could, by crossing the three river barriers in one fell swoop, seek to snatch the victor's final crown. He made the second and bolder decision, and he chose as his instrument as many of the airborne troops as could be assembled in time.

These consisted of three divisions, the 82nd and 101st, belonging to the American Army, tried troops whose mettle had been tested in the Cherbourg Peninsula, and the British 1st Airborne Division, whose valour in North Africa, in Sicily, and in southern Italy had earned for it a worthy reputation.

To them was given the task of forming a corridor of which the axis would be the Eindhoven-Veghel-Grave-Nijmegen-Arnhem road. Its formation would ensure a straight and swift advance to the gate of Germany. The bridges over the canals and rivers along the road, notably the nine-span steel bridge at Grave, that crossing the Maas-Waal Canal west of Nijmegen, the great single span steel road bridge over the Waal at Nijmegen and the bridge over the Lower Rhine at Arnhem were also to be seized.

The 101st American Division was to create that part of the corridor from Eindhoven to the outskirts of Grave ; the 82nd American Division was to establish its central section from Grave to Nijmegen and to capture the high ground south of Nijmegen overlooking the exits from the Reichswald; while the 1st British Airborne Division was to seize and hold the road bridge at Arnhem. These three divisions were, in fact, to form "a carpet of airborne troops " over which the 2nd Army might pour to break down the last barrier defending the Reich and thus gain direct access to the Ruhr.

A daylight operation is planned

The scale on which the operation was planned was larger than any which had previously been undertaken or contemplated. For the invasion of Normandy some 17,000 airborne troops had been used; for the capture of the three bridges many more must come into action. So great a number could not be transported in one lift. Moreover, the aircraft available were either Dakotas (C.47s) which are slow, unarmed and unarmoured transport aircraft not fitted with self-sealing tanks, or Stirlings, Halifaxes and Albemarles not designed to fly in daylight at a low height over hostile territory. For- and this was perhaps the most striking feature of the plan- the whole operation was to be carried out by the light of day. The Allied air forces were supreme in the air and attacks by fighters of the Luftwaffe were neither expected nor feared. The profusion of Spitfires, Thunderbolts, Mustangs, Typhoons and other fighters was so great that the protection they could give was rightly regarded as overwhelming.

There remained only the anti-aircraft defences of the enemy. As has been said, these were formidable and daily increasing. The dropping and landing zones were at extreme range and this meant that the transport and tug aircraft would have to follow the shortest possible route. The long, roaring columns would have to fly over the Dutch islands on which for the past four years the Germans had concentrated anti-aircraft batteries to prevent, if they could, the passage of day and night bombers on their way to the Ruhr.

Round the objectives themselves light flak was being concentrated in ever larger and larger quantities, Nevertheless the planners felt confident that the losses which might be incurred from anti-aircraft tire would not be so great as to imperil the operation. As it turned out, they were right, for it was only during the latter stages, when it became necessary to drop supplies to the men on the ground, that casualties became severe.

The task of the airborne troops was one with which most of them were familiar-the capture of a bridge. This is an operation in which surprise must always play an important part. In this instance all three bridges were known to be prepared for demolition with charges built into the piers and exploding apparatus housed a short distance away. They were defended by dual-purpose guns which could be used both against aircraft and troops attacking on the ground. At Nijmegen the medieval citadel called Walkliof commanded the southern approach to the bridge and had been made into a strongpoint. Finally, and this was the most important consideration of all, the airborne army, for it was nothing less- could not remain long unsupported. Two days and nights were judged to be the maximum period during which it might be able to light on its own without the aid of the heavy artillery, the tanks, and all the other weapons at the disposal of armies on the ground.

In the event of the capture of the three bridges, could the leading Corps of the Second Army then push forward with sufficient speed to relieve the airborne forces in time 'I The task was difficult. Nevertheless, it was hoped and believed that it would be able to press on, provided always that the bridges were in Allied hands. Were it to be held up, however, elaborate arrangements were made for supplying the airborne troops from the air, though, even if all supplies fell in the right place and were collected without loss, those troops would still be without heavy artillery support against an enemy who before long would have at his disposal heavy and self-propelled guns. Yet all these risks were accepted in order to breach at one blow the last natural frontiers of Germany.

The objectives at Arnhem

To the 1st Airborne Division fell the honour of taking the bridge at Arnhem. Its commander, Major-General R. E. Urquhart, C.B., DSO., in conjunction with Lieutenant-General Browning in charge of the whole operation, drew up the simplest plan which would meet the circumstances. Even this, however, involved at least two, and, as it turned out, three lifts.

All the Division was to be used, together with the Polish Parachute Brigade. One factor governed the journey to the objective and the arrival there. The German airfield at Deelen and the town of Arnhem itself were very well protected by anti-aircraft guns. Situated as it was just to the north of Arnhem, comparatively slow-flying aircraft stood no chance if they approached too near to it in daytime. It was necessary therefore for the dropping and landing zones to be well beyond the range of the guns at Deelen.

Since the country round Arnhem is for the most part well wooded, the number of suitable open fields was not very great. Four, shown on the map as Y., S., L. and X., were eventually chosen. The first three lay immediately north of the railway running through Arnhem to Utrecht, the farthest of them, Y., being about eight miles from the bridge the capture of which was the object of the expedition. The fourth zone was south of the railway and somewhat larger than the others. A fifth, close to the city itself and near the small village of Warnsborn, was chosen as the place on which supplies were to be dropped after the landing. As will become apparent in due course, for the Royal Air Force it has become a place of glorious and tragic memory.

The troops at Urquhart's disposal comprised the 1st and 4th Parachute Brigades, the 1st Air Landing Brigade, the 21st Independent Parachute Company, the 1st Air Landing Reconnaissance Squadron, the 1st and 4th Parachute Squadrons and the 9th and 261st Field Companies of the Royal Engineers, the 1st Air Landing Light Regiment and the 1st and 2nd Anti-tank Batteries of the Royal Artillery, and detachments of the Royal Army Service Corps, the Royal Corps of Signals, the Royal Army Medical Corps and the Royal Electrical and Mechanical Engineers. The total number of officers and men who were airborne was 8,969, to whom must be added 1,126 glider pilots. The 1st Parachute Brigade consisted of the 1st, 2nd and 3rd Parachute Battalions, together with Headquarters and its defence platoon.

With them was the 16th Parachute Field Ambulance. The 10th, 11th and 15,6th Parachute Battalions composed the 4th Parachute Brigade, together with a defence platoon and the

133rd Parachute Field Ambulance. The 1st Air Landing Brigade was made up of the 2nd Battalion of the South Staffordshire Regiment, the 7th Battalion of the Kings Own Scottish Borderers, the 1st Battalion of the Border Regiment, and the 181st Field Ambulance.

Since it was impossible for all these troops to land on the same day, General Urquhart's plan was to put down immediately the 1st Parachute Brigade, the 1st Air Landing Brigade, and about half the available sappers and gunners and other divisional troops. The remainder would follow on the next day.

All were to fulfil a twofold task. First and foremost, the vital road bridge at Arnhem itself must be seized, together with, if possible, the pontoon bridge three-quarters of a mile downstream, and a railway bridge some two miles still farther west as the river flows. The seizure of the main bridge was to be carried out by the 1st Parachute Brigade, which would then form a small half-circle running through the town of Arnhem, its ends firmly based to east and west on the Lower Rhine. It was hoped that they would be able to accomplish this by nightfall on D Day. As soon as the remainder of the Division landed in the morning of the second day, they were to advance on Arnhem and construct a large perimeter running round the town itself, along the high ground to the west and north-west and across the flat fields to the east and south-east.

As soon as this second perimeter was formed, the 1st Parachute Brigade would come into reserve and be reinforced by the Polish Parachute Brigade, which would drop just south of the river near the main bridge. Some of them were to land in gliders on the second day just north-east of the village of Wolf hezen. Thus by the end of the second day, when relief from the 2nd Army could be expected, there would be an outer defence round Arnhem and a solid reserve at the bridge itself. The outer perimeter would enclose the zone at Warnsborn on which fresh supplies would be dropped.

Such was the plan. Its success depended not only on the bravery and dash of the troops-these could be taken for granted-but on the inability of the Germans to react with sufficient vigour, weight and speed. That the enemy would be surprised seemed certain. How long he would take to recover from his surprise was a factor far less easy to calculate. Therein lay the risk, but it was one which Montgomery and Browning did not hesitate to take, for the victor's palm falls to him who dares the most.

CHAPTER 13

THE STRUGGLE FOR THE CROSSINGS

AT THE OUTSET ALL went well. The weather on Sunday, September 17th was good. At 10.15 in the morning, six officers and 180 men of the 21st Independent Parachute Company, under the command of Major B. A. Wilson, took off in twelve Stirlings. They were the Marker Force, and it was their duty to lay out the aids and other indications for the guidance of the main body following close behind them. They reached the dropping zones without incident, only one aircraft being fired at. A few scattered Germans were found on the ground and fifteen of them taken prisoner. Two parachutists were hit during the descent, one in his ammunition pouches, the other in his haversack. Neither was hurt. In half an hour the marks were in position, and then the first lift came in.

It was a fine sight to see the gliders carrying the 1st Air Landing Brigade and Divisional Headquarters swoop down to their appointed places, followed almost at once by the billowing parachutes of the 1st Brigade swinging down in hundreds. The drop and the glider landings were almost completely successful, ninety five per cent. of the troops reaching their rendezvous at the right place at the right time. The three battalions of parachutists and a parachute squadron of Royal Engineers forming the 1st Brigade under the command of Brigadier G. W. Lathbury, D.S.O., M.B.E., moved at once to their allotted task. It is their fortunes which must first be followed. The plan laid down for them was this : the 2nd Battalion, commanded by Lieutenant-Colonel J. D. Frost, D.S.O., M.C., a veteran of Bruneval, North Africa and Sicily, was to push on as fast as possible through the village of Heelsum and thence along the southern route, a road running close to the north bank of the Lower Rhine, until it reached the bridge, which it was to capture and hold. At the same time, the 3rd Parachute Battalion would be in the centre of the advance and move along the main Heelsum-Arnhem road to assist Frost's men by approaching the bridge from the north. The 1st Parachute Battalion was to remain with Brigade Headquarters in immediate reserve, ready to be used wherever and whenever the necessity arose.

As soon as the 2nd and 3rd Battalions had completed their immediate task, the 1st Battalion was to occupy the high ground just north of Arnhem.

To make assurance surer, most of the Air Landing Reconnaissance Squadron were to attempt a coup de main against the bridge. This, as it turned out, they were unable to do, for nearly all their transport failed to arrive.

The 2nd and 3rd Parachute Battalions, both of which had with them 2 troop of anti-tank guns and a detachment ofthe 1st Parachute Squadron R.E., moved off punctually at three p.m. through well-wooded country. Let us first follow Frost and his 2nd Battalion. In Heelsum, where they arrived soon after leaving their dropping zone, they ambushed a number of Germarn vehicles and took about twenty prisoners. The Dutch inhabitants, who turned out in force, everyone wearing " some garment or part of a garment coloured orange, some with favours, and some with orange armbands," said that there were but few Germans in Arnhem itself. The parachutists pushed on along the six miles of road which separated them from their goal, first encountering and overcoming opposition in Doorwerthsche Wood. On the way to the road bridge they had to pass to the north of the bridge carrying the railway over the river. Here trouble was caused by an armoured car and here, too, they suffered a disappointment. The railway bridge was blown just as Lieutenant Berry and a section of " C " Company reached it together with Captain E.

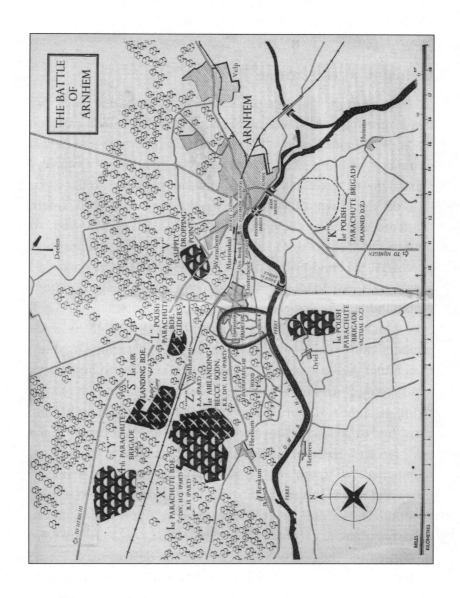

THE BATTLE OF ARNHEM

165

O'Callaghan, M.C., and a number of the 9th Field Company R.E. Some of the men were actually on the bridge when it went up. " It seemed" said Corporal Roberts of the Royal Army Medical Corps, who was present, " to curl back on us, but no one was hurt."

Collision at the bridge

The rest of the battalion pressed forward, and came under fire from some high wooded ground called Den Brink. This position was fiercely attacked by "B" Company, which took and held it at the cost of quite a few casualties. Meanwhile "A" Company skirted the position to the south, and moving close to the river, entered the town of Arnhem, where they met with small, scattered parties of Germans who were killed or captured. At eight o'clock, their eyes straining through the September dusk perceived the road bridge at last. Its half circle steel span was intact, and German transport was moving across it. The buildings commanding its northern end were immediately seized. A pill box which gave trouble was successfully deal with by a six pounder anti-tank gun and flame-throwers. Lieutenant Grayburn then attempted to rush across the bridge in order to capture its southern end. An anti aircraft gun and a German armoured car firing straight u the bridge brought this attack to naught, and Frost had to be content for the moment to hold on firmly to the northern end. He tried his best, however, to seize both ends and dispatched "B" Company, which had captured Den Brink, to cross the river lower downstream by means of a German pontoon bridge and by barge so as to outflank the southern defences of the road bridge. This they failed to do, for there were no barges and the pontoon bridge had been destroyed.

By the time Frost realized this, night had fallen ; but he held on. When dawn came, he found himself in command of a mixed force of between 600 and 700 men, with some six-pounder anti-tank guns. They were not long left in peace. About 11.30 in the morning a German column of six half-track vehicles, led by five armoured cars some fifteen to twenty yards apart, approached the bridge from the south. The armoured cars roared over it and went straight on into the town of Arnhem until they were tackled by the six-pounder anti-tank guns, which destroyed a number of them. The half-tracks were even less fortunate. When the leading vehicle arrived outside a school in which Lieutenant D. R. Simpson, M.C., R.E., with a number of Sappers, was installed, it ran into immediate trouble. Its driver and those of the rest were without the protection afforded by the armoured roofs, for these had been removed a few moments before by the six-pounders in action at the bridge itself. When, therefore, the half-tracks arrived at the school, their occupants fell an easy prey to the Sappers firing from its windows and from those of nearby houses.

The school itself stood in its own grounds and was of a square horseshoe shape, the ends of the two arms of the horseshoe being not above ten yards from the road. "I had men in one end," reported Simpson, "and Captain Mackay had some in the other. As the half-tracks came by, Corporal Simpson and Sapper Emery, whose conduct that day was outstanding, stood up and tired straight into the half-tracks with Sten and Bren guns. The range was about twenty yards." Five out of six of the half-tracks were knocked out almost at once, and created a block at the northern end of the bridge which made it impossible for any vehicles to pass. The driver of the sixth half-track, seeing the fate of the others, tried to bypass the obstacle created by the burning vehicles of his comrades, and pulled on to an asphalted path which ran under the windows of the school. His vehicle did not get far. It was hit, its crew climbed out, and sought the cover of the bushes, but were killed before reaching them."

After this unsuccessful attempt by the enemy to rush the bridge, he had recourse to continuous and heavy shell and mortar fire, which did a certain amount of damage to the houses in which Frost and his men were holding out. A heavy attack supported by several tanks and S.P. guns developed towards evening. It was driven back with the loss of one tank. Just as darkness fell, four of the houses held by the parachutists were set on fire and they had to seek other quarters.

The 3rd Battalion breaks into Arnhem

So, for a night and a day, did the 2nd Battalion hold to the vital objective.

The fortunes or, to speak more truly, the misfortunes of the 3rd and 1st Parachute Battalions must now be considered. The 3rd Parachute Battalion under Lieutenant-Colonel J. A. C. Fitch had been engaged on their approach march to the bridge for less than an hour when, at a cross-roads about a mile and three-quarters south-east of Wolf hezen and half that distance from Oosterbeek, they ran into German infantry supported by two armoured cars. "B" Company, forming the advance guard, "were rather taken aback with this first sight of armour, because the six-pounder attached to them was facing the wrong way when the cars appeared and was knocked out when trying to face round." Nevertheless, a German staff car containing four staff officers was wiped out and the armoured cars dealt with, despite a lack of Flats. After this, "C" Company advanced through "B" towards the railway with orders to find any route they could by which to reach the bridge.

This was the last seen of them by the rest of the battalion. What happened to them was this. They moved down a small by-road and the platoons soon became separated. The leading one fought an action against a captured British jeep filled with Germans and pressed on, being presently caught up by the other two platoons, which had attacked an ammunition lorry and blown it up.

At dusk all three, now much reduced in numbers, reached the railway station at Arnhem and then moved on towards the bridge, through a town deserted save, says Sergeant Mason, "for two Dutch policemen .... We walked down a main street towards the bridge. Just before reaching it, a German car was blown up by a gammon bomb thrown by the leading platoon." A confused fight then ensued, and eventually what was left of the company entered the school close to the bridge and there joined the Sappers fighting beside Frost's 2nd Battalion. On the way to the school Private McKinnon, in the hope of finding food, entered a butcher's shop of which the owner, having no meat, gave him bread, wine and cheese. "He asked," says McKinnon, "if he could bring his daughter down to see me. She was twelve years old and she had one line of English to say, 'Many happy returns after your long stay away.' "

In the meanwhile the other companies of the battalion remained near the cross-roads a mile from Oosterbeek until two hours before dawn. Their advance then continued until they reached a point in Arnhem itself near the railway, where they came under heavy and persistent fire from eighty eight mm. guns. By that time the Headquarters Company, with which marched the mortars and machine-guns and a rifle company, were cut off from those in front, whose men presently got into houses and opened fire whenever possible on the German self-propelled guns and infantry. By one p.m they were under mortar fire, which continued for the next three hours, and at three o clock Lieutenant Burwash M C, with a party of men in a carrier arrived at Battalion Headquarters, having forced a way through the intervening Germans. They arrived somewhat exhausted, having run the gauntlet of several enemy posts ; but they had with them some much needed ammunition. This was distributed with difficulty, and it was decided to break out of the houses at four p.m. and push on at any cost to the bridge. Undeterred by their already heavy losses, the battalion did so, but was soon surrounded by an ever increasing number of the enemy and split into two groups which defended themselves with vigour through the night but could make no progress.

At dawn on the next day the 19th all that were still left reached the river bank and seized a large house called the Pavillion, but could not advance from it. There they were presently joined by such elements of the 1st Battalion as remained. "Casualties were being suffered at an ever increasing rate." The Germans too were in poor case. Those on the "promenade side" of the Pavilion "were very scared and wouldn't come down to the machine gun emplacements overlooking the road and fire their guns." Some, however, were made of sterner stuff notably the crew of a Spandau firing from a point near the Junction of the pontoon bridge and the road along the river's bank. They remained at their gun and prevented any further advance.

The 1st Battalion fights through

The 1st Battalion had no better fortune. Under Lieutenant-Colonel D. T. Dobie, D.S.O., it moved off down the railway in an easterly direction following the 2nd and 3rd Battalions. "R" Company soon ran into opposition at a road junction north of the village of Wolfhezen and here a confused and desperate battle took place. The enemy were well posted on high wooded ground, and the battalion's casualties began to mount, until half "R" Company were killed or wounded. The remainder pressed on, and soon afterwards encountered five German tanks and fifteen half-track vehicles. "They could go no farther without coping with these and settled down to do so. Spasmodic but fierce fighting continued all that evening and at intervals throughout the night. " It was impossible," says Lieutenant Williams, "to make any headway. There were snipers in the woods on both sides. " What had happened was that the 2nd Battalion had preceded them along the same route earlier that afternoon, and the Germans, having been reinforced, had closed in behind them. There was very heavy opposition and there were snipers in practically every house. Individually the Germans were good, but as a body they were bad. "They weren't any good at tactics and made far more use of automatic weapons than rifles."

At first light on the 18th Lieutenant-Colonel Dobie received information that the 2nd Battalion was at the bridge and urgently needed reinforcements.

He decided to disengage his troops if he could, by-pass the enemy to the south, and move on towards the bridge. An attack by "S" Company on the left flank temporarily drove the enemy back with casualties, and the battalion pressed on a little farther, having by that time picked up the Headquarters Company of the 3rd Battalion. The fight presently shifted to some houses and a factory strongly held by the enemy near a railway bridge and a cross-roads at Mariendaal, a little suburb to the north-west of Arnhem. Here the battle raged all the morning, a first attack by "T" Company at nine o'clock being moderately successful, but a second attack on the factory failing because of the heavy fire of German twenty-mm. guns shooting northwards from the river bank. At this juncture Lieutenant-Colonel Thompson of the Light Regiment arrived and directed the fire of the seventy-five-mm. and the anti-tank guns, which were used with great effect against a pill-box in the factory. It received a direct hit and its fire was silenced. In all these engagements, or more accurately in this one long continuous struggle, heavy casualties were sustained by the enemy.

All that afternoon and evening the 1st Battalion tried to press forward, and did eventually reach the St. Elizabeth Hospital. By 6.30 p.m. its Commanding Officer was in touch with the 2nd Battalion, still holding the bridge and still urgently demanding reinforcements. By then his command was reduced to approximately a hundred men and there was hardly any ammunition. This deficit was presently remedied by the arrival of the remains of "R" Company, who had joined up with the 2nd

South Staffordshire Regiment, and a plan was made to rush forward to the bridge at nine p.m. ' At eight p.m., however, the news came that the bridge had been overrun and the attack was put off. .

Thus did the three gallant battalions of the 1st Parachute Brigade struggle to fulfil their tasks in the first vital forty-eight hours. The 2nd succeeded, for it reached and held the bridge though the conditions in which it did so increased in difficulty with every hour. The other two made determined but mostly vain efforts to reach their hard-pressed comrades ; but the main design on which the success of the operation principally depended had not been achieved. The semicircle round the bridge had not been formed and did not exist.

"Would you like to throw a bomb, sir?"

The Divisional General was an eye-witness of this fighting and himself took part in it. On landing, he made a rapid tour of his brigades and presently reached the 1st, under Brigadier Lathbury, who was with the 3rd Battalion. By then the Germans had woken up and there was considerable fire from snipers and mortars. This caused many casualties among the 3rd Battalion, and the position was such that at dusk the Major-General and the Brigadier came to the conclusion that to return to Brigade Headquarters was out of the question. They therefore remained with the 3rd Battalion, whose Headquarters had been established near a cross-roads on the main Arnhem-Heelsum road, half a mile from the suburb of Hartestein. The two men spent the night in a small house and moved off about four o'clock in the morning.

By then Urquhart's jeep had been hit and the driver knocked out. His wireless, too, was not working, and he was therefore out of touch with everyone except the troops in the immediate neighbourhood. He and the Brigadier continued to push forward into Arnhem in the wake of the 3rd Battalion in conditions which became increasingly difficult. The mortar fire was by then heavy and made it necessary to take cover in the houses. "Self propelled guns," reports the Major-General, "cruised up and down the street shooting at us and getting very aggressive." .

Between four and five in the afternoon the small party—it consisted of the Divisional Commander, Captain W. A. Taylor, Brigadier Lathbury and a subaltern-decided to move out of the house in which they had been compelled to remain for some hours. .To cover their advance smoke bombs were used. The demeanour of the senior officers was very polite. The Brigadier said to the Major-General, "Would you like to throw a bomb, sir?" He answered, "Oh, no, you'd be much better at it than I am."

Under cover of this smoke they went through some back gardens and into a street, across the end of which they ran till they reached the next street.

Here the Brigadier was hit in the back and fell to the pavement. General Urquhart and Captain Taylor picked him up and carried him into a house, where they stowed him in the cellar. While they were doing so, a German appeared at the window and Urquhart dispatched him with his revolver.

It is seldom in modern war that the Commander of a Division has an opportunity to fight the enemy at such close quarters. Leaving the Brigadier, at his urgent request, for he was partly paralysed and could not walk, they went to another house where they remained for the rest of the evening and the next night. For many hours, such were the circumstances of this peculiar battle, the Commander of the force had been unable to exercise more influence upon it than that which could be brought to bear by any private soldier engaged in it. Through the night they waited in the loft, discouraged from making an attempt to quit their-quarters by a self-propelled gun which "came along the road and parked itself in front of our door." In the early morning of the 19th they escaped during a lull, and Urquhart, leaping into a passing jeep, reached Hartestein and was at last able to resume control.

While he had been thus lost, his place had been taken by Brigadier P. H. W. Hicks, D.S.O., MC., whose every effort was directed towards concentrating as many men as possible in the area of the vital bridge. How the 1st Parachute Brigade endeavoured to seize and hold it has already been told. Their efforts were later seconded by "B" and "D" Companies of the 2nd Battalion of the South Staffordshire Regiment under the command of Colonel W. D. McCardie. They had landed by gliders at the Reijer's Camp landing zone. The remainder of the Battalion was to come in with the second lift.

After a sharp engagement near Mariendaal to the immediate west of Arnhem, the two companies, with a detachment of the 9th Field Company R.E., eventually got through and entered the town, one at about seven in the evening of the 18th, the other about midnight. There they made contact with what remained of the 1st and 3rd Parachute Battalions.

The gliders arrive on schedule The remainder of the first lift, consisting of the 1st Battalion of the Border Regiment and the 7th Battalion of the King`s Own Scottish Borderers, arrived on schedule. It was their duty to seize and hold the landing grounds and dropping zones, so that the second lift, due to land on the next day, might do so in safety. Lieutenant-Colonel R. Payton-Reid, commanding the Borderers, paints a dry picture of the flight and the arrival. "We started off," he says, "in a certain amount of low mist, which caused some of the gliders to release over England. However, when we got over the Channel it was bright and clear. We had a good trip, not bumpy. Three of my gliders went down in the sea. They were all picked up in fifteen minutes by the Air Sea Rescue Service. It was interesting to see the Dutch islands all flooded completely, except for a few buildings sticking up out of the water. There was no flak.

"The first glider came down at 1.30 and we all moved off at

three o'clock. Everything was unloaded by then. We had no local help. There were one or two crashed gliders. We couldn't get out the motor bikes and one anti-tank gun. A lot of the gliders' undercarriages came up through the bottom because we landed on very soft ground. Eight gliders didn't arrive, otherwise we were complete, just over 700 men and forty officers. The battalion landed to the tune of its regimental march, 'The Blue Bonnets over the Border,' played by a piper who continued to march up and down the rendezvous till all the men had reached it."

Throughout the afternoon and the night the Borderers held the dropping zones, being thrice unsuccessfully attacked by the Germans.

happened to the Border Regiment covering the dropping zones to the south- those to the north were held by the Borderers- was very similar. They suffered to a certain degree from mortar fire, which by the end of the 18th had destroyed all the vehicles belonging to "B" Company.

Whether the course of the battle in the first twenty-four hours would have been changed, had it been possible for Major-General Urquhart to use these two Battalions of the Air Landing Brigade to reinforce the hard-pressed 1st Parachute Brigade, must at present remain a matter of conjecture. The tenacious resistance of the Germans on the high ground west and north o Arnhem proved too strong for the comparatively lightly armed parachute battalions to overcome. Had more troops been thrown into the battle success might well have been achieved, but it was precisely this possibility which was denied to Urquhart. At any cost he had to hold the landing zone so that his reinforcements might be able to land without incurring prohibitive casualties. At the crucial moment, therefore, on the afternoon c that September Sunday, he lacked just that added punch which might have knocked down the German guard. Had the whole Division been carried in one lift, the Border Regiment and the Borderers would not have had to play a comparatively static role in the first and all- important twenty-for hours, nor would the South Staffords have had to go into action with on half their strength.

The impossibility of arranging for all units to arrive together was or reason why the 1st Airborne Division failed to hold the crossings of the Lowe Rhine. Another was also to become apparent in the first twenty-four hours. The plan provided for the arrival of the second lift containing the balance of the Division at latest by ten in the morning of Monday, the 18th. That day broke fine and clear over Arnhem, and the spirits of the men fighting in its streets and in the woods around its trim houses were uplifted when they saw the bright sun and the clear sky. Major Wilson was soon busy putting out more markers, for he and his men heard the sound of aircraft approaching. They had been told that any they might see or hear would be friendly ; but, as they were completing their task, they looked up and saw a numb of Messerschmitt 109s diving upon them. They leapt hastily for cover. The minutes began to go by, and then the hours, and still the second lift did not appear, for on this side of the Channel cloud and foggy conditions prevented combinations from taking off till after midday. It was not until between three and four in the afternoon that they arrived in the landing area. This delay of several vital hours still further complicated a situation which was becoming increasingly difficult.

The second lift comes in

The arrival of the second lift was accomplished with but few casualties. They had left in "very filthy weather indeed, low cloud and rain," but after a while it improved and, says Major R. Cain of the South Staffords, who was soon to win a Victoria Cross, "a little while after mid-Channel I saw the coastline of Holland in front. It was a buff-fawny colour, with white and grey streaks .... The next thing l recognised was the Rhine. Then we got flak puffs all round us and bits of tracer. l got the fellows strapped in. Geary, the glider pilot ... put her into a dive approach. It seemed to be about treetop level when he pulled her out straight and shouted 'Hold tight' and we landed in a ploughed field .... We got out and took up all-round protective positions .... All the area was divided up into square fields with little tree-lined earth roads dividing them. It was very neat and very square. The trees were elms. I could hear very little firing and what there was a long way off. There was no other activity."

The enemy were, however, more active than on the first day. It was under heavy fire that Lance-Sergeant Maddocks of the South Staffords, for example, had to saw off the tail of his glider in order to unload a Vickers gun, and Flight-Sergeant Carter, one of twenty-five instructors from the Parachute Training School who that day flew with some of their erstwhile pupils, found himself dispatching an officer, a sergeant-major and sixteen men of the 10th Parachute Battalion from a burning Dakota twenty miles or more from the dropping zone. This task he accomplished without loss, and himself jumped with the American crew whose' pilot, Lieutenant Tucker, remained at the controls to the last possible moment and thus ensured a safe drop.

Carter joined the advanced elements of the leading Corps of the Second Army Corps and was back at his task of instructing four days later.

Generally speaking, however, the second lift arrived without undue difficulty. A few gliders did not. One, carrying Lieutenant A. T. Turrell and his men, was shot down between Nijmegen and Arnhem but succeeded in making a good landing. Thirty Dutchmen helped to unload the glider, among them a girl who to do so abandoned her search for a green parachute among those lying about. She wanted it, she said, to make a dress of that colour. Under the guidance of a Dutch priest and a local official the party set oh" for the Division, who were the other side, of the Rhine. On the Way they met with six Germans whom they disarmed and locked in the local gaol, after first making them take off their uniforms and put on civilian clothes.

All eventually reached the neighbourhood of Arnhem by crossing the Lower Rhine in a ferry.

Once the second lift was down, Brigadier Hicks, still in command of the Division in the continued absence of the Major-General, decided at any cost to reinforce those holding the bridge. He had some knowledge of what was happening from the Dutch inhabitants of Arnhem, who showed the greatest courage and resolution in keeping him informed. The telephone exchange had been taken over by members of the Resistance Movement, who passed messages whenever possible. A tall, cadaverous Dutchman volunteered, provided he could be fitted out with a uniform, to take a jeep to the bridge with ammunition. The 1st and 3rd Battalions of the 1st Parachute Brigade were disintegrating in the streets of Arnhem ; they must be reinforced. In order to do so, Hicks instructed the 2nd South Staffords to move along the road beside the river, while the 11th Parachute Battalion, forming part of the 4th Parachute Brigade which had just landed, was to take the northern route so as to effect the same object. Neither the Parachute Battalion nor the South Staffords could get farther than the St. Elizabeth Hospital and a building called the Monastery, both some distance from the bridge, though they started with comparative ease.

"We moved off in the proper order of march," says Major Cain, "and I remember checking several men as they went past for things like not having their bayonets fixed. It was so like an exercise that I did this automatically."

They passed through the suburb of Wolf hezen, badly smashed by the medium bombers of the 2nd Tactical Air Force two nights before, and then found themselves in an outer suburb of "extremely attractive houses gaily painted in every sort of colour. They were bright colours, but somehow they looked right. These houses were set back in the woods and were without the railings and fences round the gardens that we have in

England. The people . . . stood in the road, greeting us. They offered us water and apples, which I think was all they had. The street we went down might have been the outskirts of any English town, but it was cleaner. There were one or two factories. The houses stood in rows but were not detached. I saw our troops talking to an attractive blonde through a window. We were very confident, then."

The South Staffords ran into heavy fire on the western outskirts of Arnhem and were eventually challenged near the junction of the road with the railway running up from Nijmegen. Night had long since fallen, for they had taken thirteen hours to cover three miles ; but their challenger, who was a glider pilot, cheered them by saying that they were now only two miles from the bridge ; he added, however, that the road was under machine-gun fire.

At a conference between the Commanders of the reinforcing Battalions and Lieutenant-Colonel O. Dobie, D.S.O., commanding the remnants of the 1st and 3rd Parachute Battalions still fighting in Arnhem, it was decided to continue the advance at first light, the South Staffords on the left, the parachute troops on the right, nearest the river.

Soon they reached the St, Elizabeth Hospital, marked by "a statue of a female wearing a crown and flowing robes, set in the wall," and a large Geneva flag, and the leading platoons of the South Staffords pushed on 400 yards farther east and by 6.30 a.m. had captured the Monastery.

To advance farther was impossible, for the pressure of the enemy was increasing every moment. So close indeed were the Germans that to use mortars was very difficult: "they were shooting almost straight up in the air." The attackers, now thrown on the defensive, were without anti-tank guns, which could not be brought up because of the heavy fire on the road behind. There were, however, a number of Piats available.

To advance further was impossible, for the pressure of the

enemy was increasing every moment. So close indeed were the Germans that to use mortars was very difficult : "they were shooting almost straight up in the air." The attackers, now thrown on the defensive, were without anti-tank guns, which could not be brought up because of heavy fire on the road behind. There were, however, a number of Piats available.

For three hours the German attacks were beaten off, largely by the efforts of Lieutenant Georges Dupenois, Major Buchanan and Major Cain. "When a tank appeared we got four Brens firing on it with tracers. That shut its lid up, because the commander couldn't stand up in the turret. As soon as we'd let off a Piat at it, we'd move back and then the German shells would explode below us." About 11.30 in the morning the ammunition for the Piats gave out, the position was overrun, and what remained of the heroic South Staffords withdrew to a wooded dell just west of the Monastery.

It became a shambles. The German tanks came up and fired right into it, causing heavy casualties. "We could hear the call 'Stretcher bearer' all the time. There was no effective fire going back against these beasts because we had no ammunition."

Despite its heavy losses the 1st Parachute Battalion still had fight in it. It sought to share in the advance, and Major Perrin-Brown led "T" Company, the parachute war cry "Whoa, Mohammed!" bursting from their throats, in a bayonet charge which reduced their strength to eight men. A little later Major Timothy led "R" Company in a similar charge and fought on till only six were left. Their pertinacity had brought them to within a thousand yards of the bridge, and they could do no more. The few left, nearly all wounded, presently fell with their Colonel into the enemy's hands.

Fighting to establish an outer perimeter

While these efforts were being made to reinforce Frost at the bridge, the rest of the Air Landing Brigade and the 4th Parachute

Brigade, which had come in with the second lift, were seeking to establish the outer perimeter and thus fulfil the second part of the original plan. To do so the 4th Parachute Brigade, under Brigadier J. W. Hackett, D.S.O., M.B.E., M.C., assaulted the high ground which had proved such a grim obstacle to its original attackers, the 1st Brigade. They had no better success, for by now the Germans had completely recovered from the initial surprise and, what was worse, had been reinforced. The arrival of the second lift in the afternoon instead of the morning had given the enemy six hours' respite, and he had taken all possible advantage of it.

Nor were the Border Regiment and the King's Own Scottish Borderers north of the railway more successful. The second had lost a certain number of men holding the dropping and landing zones ; but so effectively had they accomplished their task that the casualties among the 4th Parachute Brigade on landing were very small. At seven o'clock in the evening the Borderers moved forward to occupy the positions allotted to them in the high ground north-west of Arnhem. They reached them with difficulty in the middle of the night and held on the next day, being joined in the afternoon by a number of Poles who had landed in gliders near Wolf hezen and suffered very heavily in doing so.

While the Commanding Officer of the Borderers was conferring with the Brigadier at Brigade Headquarters, the Germans launched an attack. On returning, he says, "I found the hell of a battle going on." He had just been ordered to withdraw his battalion south of the railway to avoid being taken in the rear, but, before he could do so, he had to beat off this attack. "This we did successfully," he reports, "Major Cochran, who was afterwards killed, killing twenty of the enemy, and Drum-Major Tate the same number. . . All the Boches who weren't killed turned and went back into the woods, so I took the opportunity of going south." Eventually the battalion, now reduced to fewer than 300 men, got into a position in two large houses near a small wood just south of the railway.

The Border Regiment were farther to the east, and "B" Company, in the village of Renkum, held out successfully against heavy attacks. "We got ourselves into houses and a factory," says Lieutenant Skilton, and in the morning the Germans started walking round the town. We waited till they got together in the main street into a number of nice little groups. Then we opened fire and killed thirty-five at very short range. That rather upset them, but they returned to the attack, and our position was very heavily shelled with mortars and self-propelled guns, whose fire destroyed most of buildings we were in, and all our transport." "D" Company was equally tenacious and beat off attack after attack launched against the landing it was defending throughout a period of thirty-six hours.

Major Wilson's independent Parachute Company and the glider pilots also shared in this heavy fighting. Having laid out the markers for second lift, the Independent Company then met with snipers from an S.S. Battalion and immediately attacked them. Very soon "the Germans in their sniper's suits crawled out of their slits and grovelled on the ground begging for mercy. They were terrified to see men wearing red berets and had to be violently persuaded to their feet." The assaults of the enemy continued however, especially during the night and on the morning of the third and "whenever the Germans attacked they all shouted to each other, it being obviously part of the drill, and above their shouts could be heard the voices of the N.C.Os. cursing and swearing and urging them on to battle. This shouting sounded eerie in the woods."

The glider pilots, after having safely brought the troops to the battle, now as heavily engaged as their passengers. Those who had flown in the first lift helped to hold the landing zones and then, when the second lift had come in, fought side by side with the King's Own Scottish Borderers and eventually formed part of the defence of Divisional Headquarters, established at

Hartestein. They were soon heavily engaged, and with them were Troops of the 4th Parachute Squadron R.E., one of whose officers, Captain H. F. Brown, earned a Military Cross for the manner in which he lead the sappers fighting as infantry. Thus after two and a half days of bitter, unceasing strife, the first phase ended. The northern end of the bridge been taken and was still in our hands ; but the rest of the design had awry.

A confused and bitter struggle

That this was so had been realized by Major-General Urquhart who, soon as he had escaped from the house on the outskirts of Arnhem, had taken over command once more. Now he was faced with a difficult and urgent decision. Was it still possible to carry out all or part or none of the plan ? The Air Landing Brigade had established itself more or less in position originally chosen, west and south-west of Arnhem. For sixty hours the 1st Parachute Brigade had been heavily involved in the town and the position of its battalions was very obscure except that, as far as was known Frost and his men were still at the bridge. The 4th Parachute Brigade, which was to hold that part of the perimeter comprising the northern approaches to Arnhem had been unable to capture their positions. How could what remained of it best be used ?

Urquhart soon decided that it was quite out of the question to attempt to put it north of the railway, in other words to create that outer perimeter which should include the town within its embrace. On the afternoon third day, therefore, the Brigade was ordered to disengage and to move of the railway so as to occupy, if possible, the high ground between Oosterbeek and the town ; but even this task proved impossible. With staccato clarity the diary of the 156th Parachute Battalion, one of its units, tells why. On the day before, in twenty-four hours two of its companies, striving to make headway, had been cut to pieces in the woods just north of the railway.

"0830 hours. ' A ' Company put in an attack on the line of defence on the road running from Arnhem to Utrecht. The company met very heavy opposition including S.P. guns and armoured cars after suffering heavy casualties, including all officers. "0900 hours. ' B ' Company put in an attack on the same line moving round the north of 'A' Company and met with the same heavy opposition. Its commander was wounded and heavy casualties were sustained."

By the afternoon of September 19th, therefore, the battalion was already gravely reduced in numbers, when "orders were received from Headquarters to move to the area of the hotel at Wolfhezen in fifteen minutes' time. Owing to the speed of this move and the fact that the enemy were attacking, the battalion got divided and "S" Company and half of "B" and "C" Companies moved along the north side of the railway. They were attacked and overrun during the night, and except for the Quartermaster and six men, have not been heard of or seen since."

Sergeant T. C. Bentley of the 10th Parachute Battalion, equally involved in this action, is more explicit. "We were given orders," he says, " to leave the wood. It was every man for himself, for by then we were all split up. The top of the wood was occupied by fifty or sixty Germans .... Sergeant Sunley and Sergeant Houghton were terrific. We ran across a playing field and found several men showing yellow triangles. We understood that they were Poles .... We had by then lost about two-thirds, but the men were still in good heart though they had no more support weapons."

What happened to the 10th and 156th Parachute Battalions is typical of the fate suffered by the rest of the Brigade. There was no respite given or demanded. Captain L. E. Queripel of the 10th Parachute Battalion was especially conspicuous. After carrying a wounded sergeant to cover under heavy fire, he was himself hit in the face but, undeterred, continued to lead his men. A strong-point composed of a captured British anti-tank gun and two machine-guns was a cause of trouble and casualties. Captain Queripel attacked it alone, killed its occupants, and recaptured the gun. Later that day he was again wounded, but insisted on covering the withdrawal of his men from a position which had been untenable for several hours but had none the less been held. In so doing he exhausted the ammunition of his automatic pistol and threw every grenade he could find at the enemy. He did not rejoin his men and was not seen again. For these deeds he was awarded the Victoria Cross.

Captain R. Temple was at Brigade Headquarters, which, after losing all its transport, had taken to a hollow south of the railway. "We spent," he says, "most of the day there being attacked all the time .... At one stage we thought the Germans wanted to surrender, and they thought that we did.... By Wednesday evening the strength of the Brigade was about 250. We were practically out of ammunition and the Germans were still attacking."

Eventually what remained of the Brigade reached the area of Divisional Headquarters ; but by then it was not more than 150 strong, and it was obvious that the task given it was beyond its strength. Urquhart, therefore, with great reluctance, was forced to take a decision which meant the abandonment of all the troops near the bridge, the seizure of which had been the main object of the operation. The virtual destruction of the 4th Parachute Brigade in the woods north and north-west of Arnhem, the virtual disappearance of the 1st Parachute Brigade in the town itself, and the heavy losses sustained by the Air Landing Brigade left him, indeed, no choice.

He decided to form a perimeter round the suburb of Oosterbeek and there hold out until the long expected relief from the 2nd Army arrived, using for this purpose the remains of the 4th Brigade together with any other troops available.

Strange episodes of the battle

The accounts which have come to hand of the fierce lighting of those first days, though confused and incomplete, for many who took part in them are dead and many were captured, show the indomitable spirit of these airborne troops, their skill and high heart, and their strange cheerfulness in conditions of the most adverse kind. At one point the Germans brought up a loudspeaker which first played jazz music and then urged the "Gentlemen of the 1st Airborne Division to remember your wives and sweethearts at home." It ended by enumerating a list of the more important officers alleged to be already prisoners, and by promising a heavy attack by an entire Panzer Division. "This monologue," says Captain H. F. Brown, M.C., R.E., "was not allowed to be heard for long, for it was greeted by abuse, catcalls, whistles and occasional bursts from a Bren gun. We all thought it was a great joke." A Piat being fired in the direction of the loudspeaker, "there was a big bang and it stopped."

Major Gordon Sherriff of the King's Own Scottish Borderers, going round the posts with his Colonel, ran into someone who spoke German. The first to recover from his surprise was the Major who, though suffering from a wound, tackled the man with his bare hands and killed him. The Colonel whom he accompanied on that occasion was Payton-Reid, whose stout exploits and those of his battalion have already been mentioned.

An officer of the South Staffords left Arnhem for the slightly less unhealthy neighbourhood of Oosterbeek by rolling away from a tank which had stopped within Fifty yards of him. Its commander was "standing up as bold as anything in the turret, wearing black gloves and with hand held glasses in his hand " ; but he failed to see the British officer, who rolled over and over slowly away from the trench in which he had been sitting till he reached a wall. This he climbed, and then fell twenty feet into the courtyard of the hospital beyond and "quietly passed out for ten minutes. Then I got up and moved through the back of the hospital and so out of Arnhem. "

For the first few days, and until reinforcements reached the area, the confusion in the enemy's ranks caused by the arrival of the parachutists was very great. Individual Germans did not know what was happening, or even that any airborne attack had been made. Having set off that morning on his rounds to pay the troops, a German field cashier, for example, drove in a sidecar into the position of the Independent Parachute Company with a bag full of Reichsmark notes, while a German lorry driver, wearing a Dutch farmer's smock, took his vehicle past another of our posts. As he had forgotten to take off his steel helmet he did not get by ; the truck was fired on and, since it contained ammunition, exploded.

Then there was the episode of the Piat, the company cook and the German tank. A hospital had been established in a large house in a street where fighting was fierce and continuous, the enemy being in some of the houses and our men in others including one next door to the hospital. The German commander sent its garrison a message by the regimental doctor to the effect that, if they did not evacuate the house, he would blow them to pieces with his tanks, of which he had three. The British officer in command replied that he was prepared to move if the German promised not to enter the hospital.

At the same time he told his company cook to slip out by the back door and fire on the leading German tank with a Piat. The cook, Dixon by name, knew more of pots and pans than of Piats, but his first shot hit the back of the tank and exploded the ammunition it carried. The Germans at once retreated and ceased to menace the hospital. Episodes such as these stand out from the dull background of unceasing danger, utter lack of sleep and slow torment from hunger and thirst. All these and more were steadfastly endured. Already the 2nd Army was two days overdue and no relief was in sight ; yet the Division held on.

The valiant defenders of the bridge

Before recounting the last stand round the village of Oosterbeek, We must return to the bridge and the men who had captured it by nightfall of the first day, and who still held on with grim tenacity long after all hopes of relief or reinforcement had vanished. The destruction of the German armoured cars and half-track vehicles which sought to cross the bridge and enter Arnhem on the morning of the 18th showed the enemy that the Parachutists were strongly established and in force. He therefore began to mortar the houses and positions on or near the bridge ; these were held by the 2nd Battalion and remnants of the 3rd, supported by elements of the Headquarters of the 1st Parachute Brigade, of the Royal Engineers, the R.A.M.C. and R.A.S.C., of the Light Regiment of Artillery and one troop of anti-tank guns. This mortar fire continued as long as there were any airborne troops in the area.

In the afternoon of the 18th an enemy attack succeeded in driving some of the Brigade defence platoon out of their houses, but the two German tanks leading it were eventually knocked out, one by a six-pounder, the other by a Piat ; and just before dark, four houses were set on fire and their garrisons had therefore to leave them. All through that day there had been many rumours that the 1st and 3rd Battalions would arrive with much needed reinforcements, but by late afternoon no one had appeared and hope died, to be revived, however, by the news that the South Staffordshires and the 11th Parachute Battalion were fighting their way towards the bridge.

In an endeavour to deal with Frost and his men before their arrival, the Germans, about sunset, formed up for an infantry attack but were forestalled by the parachutists. Shouting their battle-cry, "Whoa, Mohammed!" they charged the enemy with the bayonet and the Germans fled.

After an uneasy night with many alarums and excursions the

captors of the bridge prepared at dawn on the 19th to deal with further counter-attacks. These did not develop immediately, for at first the enemy contented himself with heavy mortaring and shelling, the shells being fired by tanks which had crept up to a position close to the river bank. This fire lasted throughout the morning until Captain A. Frank dealt with the tanks by means of Piats, scoring three direct hits but using all the remaining ammunition.

The German tanks limped away, and about this time Lieutenant McDerment recaptured a house from which he and his platoon had been driven. The battle swayed this way and that ; but in general, despite the fierce efforts of the enemy, the defenders of the bridge held on and did not falter, not even when a Tiger tank moved down the road just before dark and pumped shells into each house in turn. The casualties it caused included Father Egan, MC., who had served from the outset with the Brigade, and Major A.D. Tatham-Warter, both of whom were wounded but remained in action. The method used by the defence was to stalk the tanks by moving from room to room through the houses, knocking holes in the partition walls in order to do so, and thus getting close enough to fire a Piat or throw a gammon bomb.

It was in this way that Lieutenant Simpson knocked out a tank close to the house in which he was posted. Its crew got out and "crept along the wall till they came to a halt beneath the window where I was crouching. I dropped a grenade on them and that was that. I held it for two seconds before I let it drop."

In the morning of the next day Frost, who was in command of the whole force, was badly wounded and the active defence was taken over by Major C. F. H. Gough, M.C., commanding the Reconnaissance Squadron, though Frost continued to do all he could to bear a share in the fighting. To report his presence and the situation at the bridge, Gough spoke to the Divisional Commander, using not wireless, for all the sets were out of order, but the Arnhem telephone system. The exchange was held and operated by Dutch patriots, but to make sure that any German who might be listening in would not be able to identify him, Gough referred to himself throughout as "the man who goes in for funny weapons."

The final stand at the bridge

By midnight the defence was "greatly weakened." The 2nd Battalion, commanded first by Major Wallis and, after his death, by Major Tatham-Warter, whose conduct was exemplary even amid so much gallantry, had suffered heavy casualties ; so had its supporting troops, among whom must be numbered the signallers fighting as infantrymen under Captain B. Briggs.

Ammunition was running short, and the key house commanding the north end of the bridge had been burnt down. The Germans posted in houses farther back nearer the town, though making no attempt to infiltrate, kept the whole area of the defence under more or less continuous small arms and automatic fire. The number of wounded had now reached serious proportions. They were lying in the cellars of a house, attended by two Royal Army Medical Corps doctors, Captains J. Logan, D.S.O., and D. Wright, M.C., who did particularly tine work in dreadful conditions and remained with them to the end. The order to surrender the wounded was given by Colonel Frost after the house had been set on fire. Wednesday, September 20th, brought no relief. By then the Force had been burnt out of its original positions on or near the bridge and was lighting in the ruins close to and beneath it. Presently German tanks were able to move across the bridge from north to south, for the six-pounders, sighted to cover it, were under small arms fire and could not be manned. Aircraft also played a part in the German attacks, and a Messerschmitt 109, diving on the position, hit the steeple of a nearby church and crashed. Nevertheless, the defence was still maintained and hopes were still high, for news had been received that the 2nd Army would attack the south end of the bridge that afternoon at five p.m.

By now those of the defenders who were not beneath the bridge were holding slit trenches hastily dug in the gardens of the houses from which they had been driven by fire. The spirit of the defence is best exemplified by the following wireless dialogue which was overheard.

Captain Briggs : The position is untenable. Can I have permission to withdraw?

Frost : If it is untenable you may withdraw to your original position.

Captain Briggs : Everything is comfortable. I am now going in with bayonets and grenades.

The final stand was made, first in a warehouse, and then underneath the bridge, the total number still capable of fighting being about 110 men and five or six officers. The position was shelled by a German tank and armoured car, but they were unable to hit that part of the underside of the bridge where the defence was holding out. It was at this juncture that Lieutenant Grayburn, whose valour earned him a Victoria Cross which he did not live to receive, led a series of counter-attacks, in one of which Germans laying charges to blow the bridge were killed and the charges torn out. Every time a patrol went out it suffered casualties, and with each hour the situation became more and more hopeless. There was no more ammunition, there had been no food for a long time, and hardly a man but was wounded. The very ground on which the defenders stood or crouched was constantly seared by flames from the burning houses about it, and no man could remain there and live.

So in the end the gallant remnant were dispersed or captured.

CHAPTER 14

THE BATTLE OF THE PERIMETER

WHILE THIS RESOLUTE and increasingly desperate stand was being made at the bridge, the fighting had veered from Arnhem itself to the village of Oosterbeek, which forms its western suburb. Here by Wednesday, September 20th, Major-General Urquhart had by strenuous effort at last established a perimeter of defence. The western half consisted of a detachment of glider pilots, the remnants of three companies of the Border Regiment, some Poles and a number of Royal Engineers. It was commanded by Brigadier Hicks.

The eastern half was made up of three glider pilot detachments, the Borderers, the Reconnaissance Squadron, the 21st Independent Parachute Company, elements of the Royal Army Service Corps who had abandoned the care of vehicles and stores and were fighting stoutly as infantry, all that remained of the 156th and 10th Parachute Battalions, and "Lonsdale Force," called after its Commander, Major R. T. H. Lonsdale, D.S.O., M.C., and made up of elements of the 1st, 3rd and 11th Parachute Battalions and the 2nd South Staffords. This eastern half was put under Brigadier Hackett, soon to be badly wounded. His place was taken by Lieutenant-Colonel I. Murray, the Commander of No. I Wing of the Glider Pilot Regiment. Such artillery as remained was concentrated north and south of Oosterbeek Church.

In this shrinking perimeter, of which the centre was roughly at Hartestein, where Headquarters were situated, the Division held out until the order to withdraw was received on Monday,

September 25th, and obeyed that night.

Within it all ranks fought with a gallant tenacity, equalled perhaps, but never surpassed by any soldiers of the British Army either now or at any other time in its long and honourable history. Here are a few of the many "moving accidents by Hood and field" and "hairbreadth escapes the imminent deadly breach" which occurred to every officer and man during those last grim days. There were the adventures of Lonsdale and his men near Oosterbeek Church. Lonsdale had been hit by a fragment of anti-aircraft shell just before jumping, but did not allow this handicap to interfere with his duties. Repeated enemy attacks on the church were beaten off, until his force was reduced to one Piat and one bomb. Then he withdrew to a nearby wood and there held out to the end. Among his men was the gallant Sergeant Walker of the South Staffords, who knocked out two tanks and was then wounded but, disregarding this mishap, seized a Bren gun and with it halted dead a German counter-attack, only to fall a victim shortly afterwards to the fire of a German tank.

North of the church Major R. Cain of the South Staffords and his company were fighting an equally stout battle. Soon after their arrival, and before occupying their new positions, they found a laundry where the men "had a wash and put on clean shirts which they found lying about."

Thus refreshed they took their stand on the high ground to the left of the church, a severe edifice with "a funeral inscription on the wall with some cherubs blowing trumpets round it." There they were soon repeatedly attacked by tanks and self-propelled guns, of which they knocked out some three or four.

A self-propelled gun which came into action every morning and afternoon was particularly troublesome. Cain determined to destroy it and fired some fifty bombs at it, his fire being directed by Captain Ian Meikle, who continued to do so till he was killed. Cain eventually entered a little shed with-a Piat and two bombs, put his head round a corner of the door and seeing the gun, "fired at the thing and the bomb went off underneath it." The last shot of the gun blew the shed to pieces just after Cain had left it. Hardly had he disposed of the self-propelled gun when a tank came up the road. He crept towards it, waited till it was less than a hundred yards away, and then fired the Piat. The tank fired back immediately, and "this raised a huge cloud of dust and smoke. As soon as I could see the outline of the tank I let it have another. This also raised a lot of dust again, and through it I saw the crew of the tank baling out." They were dealt with by a Bren gun.

Cain fired a last shot to make sure, but the bomb burst prematurely in the muzzle of the Piat, wounding him in the face, perforating an eardrum and giving him two black eyes.

"'I' the imminent, deadly breach"

Major F. A. S. Murray. of the Glider Pilot Regiment carried on the fight until wounded in the throat. Undaunted he led a successful counter-attack, and only then went to hospital, where he soon found himself in enemy hands. This did not suit him : after having his wound dressed, he walked out, "quite unarmed and in broad daylight," and made his way back to the Division. Major Bush of the 3rd Parachute Battalion behaved in similar fashion, breaking out of captivity to rejoin and then command a section of the perimeter. This, though again wounded, he held till the order to withdraw came.

It cannot too often be pointed out that the enemy mortar fire was of the most deadly kind. Our own, though not so heavy for lack of ammunition, also did great execution. The mortars maintained in action by Lieutenant H. R. Holman of the Border Regiment were especially well fought until all were destroyed together with most of their crews. When the last round had been tired and last mortar silenced, Holman collected all who were still on their feet and they fought on as infantry.

Captain R. R. Temple, G.S.O. III to the 4th Parachute

Brigade, fought for most of the time one-handed, his right arm having been smashed on the morning of the 20th. His shooting with a revolver held in his left hand was "most accurate." Captain J. W. Walker, a gunner, ended as adjutant to Payton-Reid, taking over his new duties on return from a two-day visit to hospital, whither he had been sent by a bullet which had perforated his steel helmet and the top of his head. Sergeant J. N. Smith kept his Bren gun in action after an enemy shell had knocked down the house on top of him.

Signalman R. M. Duguid had two jeeps shot under him, the second of which he repaired, under heavy fire. Private J. Steele of the Border Regiment became a purveyor of gammon bombs, retrieving these dangerous and useful weapons from a container which had been seen to fall in a sniper-haunted wood, just before an enemy tank attack developed.

The non-combatants vied with the fighting men in gallantry and devotion to duty. Private J. C. Proudfoot, a stretcher-bearer, "repeatedly we out into the open in full view to dress the casualties and drag them safety" : Captain R. T. Watkins, Chaplain to the 1st Parachute Battalion, was always "where the need was most great" and saved the lives of large numbers of the wounded. These deeds, chosen at random from files bright with similar reports on the actions of men equally brave, embroider a deathless tale and explain how it was that Oosterbeek continued to be defended long after it had by all the canons of war become untenable. The account them must end with the most remarkable of all, the exploits of Lance-Sergeant J. D. Baskeyfield of the South Staffordshire Regiment.

On September 20th, not long after the perimeter was formed, a fierce attack on Oosterbeek was launched by the enemy. Sergeant Baskeyfield was in command of a section manning a six-pounder anti-tank gun. Fighting it with the utmost "coolness and daring" they destroyed two Tiger tanks and a self propelled gun, holding their fire to make sure of success until the enemy were less than a hundred yards off. The sergeant and his crew did not escape unscathed. All were killed or wounded, Baskeyfield being badly hit in the leg. Refusing to be carried to the Regimental Aid Post, he remained alone with the gun and soon afterwards repelled a second and even fiercer armoured attack. "By this time" reports his Commanding Officer "his activity was the main factor in keeping the enemy tanks at bay. Of this the enemy themselves soon became aware for their fire destroyed his gun ; but the sergeant crawled- he could not walk- under intense fire to another close at hand, of which all the crew were dead, and brought single handed into action. He fired but two rounds and caused a self propelled gun to come to an abrupt halt. But the tank behind it fired and Sergeant Baskeyfield fell dead beside his second six pounder. For these deeds he was awarded a posthumous Victoria Cross, and his best epitaph is to be found in the words with which the citation ends. "During the remaining days at Arnhem stories of his valour were a constant inspiration to all ranks."

The tenacity of the gunners

In all this heavy fighting the guns under the Commander of the Roy Artillery, Lieutenant-Colonel R. G. Loder-Symonds D.S.O., M.C., played a conspicuous part. Fifteen out of sixteen of the seventy-five mm. guns arrived safely with the first lift, and their numbers grew to twenty-one out a possible twenty four after the second lift had come in. They were put to the most strenuous use, on the first day firing forty rounds a gun, on the second fifty ; but shortage of ammunition made it impossible to maintain this rate in the later stages. Most of the guns were served in the firing line itself, and sometimes in advance of it. Their fire was directed by a number of forward observation officers posted in various points of vantage. Here Lieutenant J W Widdicombe held on for twenty-four hours directing a battery which broke up a heavy attack of the enemy, though the building on which he stood was shot to pieces all round him and he was compelled to continue his task perched on its wreckage.

"C" troop of the 2nd Battery was attacked on September 24th by a Tiger tank and a self-propelled gun at a range of 150 yards. The crews were prevented from firing their guns by heavy machine-gun fire, but Lieutenant A. Donaldson, with Lance-Bombardier Dickson, ran across a hundred yards of open ground and manned a six-pounder anti-tank gun, of which the crew had been killed. This the two men brought into action, but after firing eight or nine rounds the gun received a direct hit from the tank, which stunned Donaldson. On coming to, he and his bombardier made their way back to one of the guns of "C" troop and maintained it in action until all the ammunition was expended. Dickson then sought and found a Piat and with this weapon went on with the battle.

That same day Sergeant Daly of "B" troop temporarily dazed a Tiger tank with two shots tired at a range of a hundred yards. A second Tiger, attempting to pass the first, jolted it, whereupon it started into life again and opened heavy machine-gun fire against the sergeant and his anti-tank gun.

Everyone dived for cover, but Sergeant Daly crawled back to the gun, laid it, and sent the tank up in flame with his first round. Such deeds as these show the tenacity with which the guns were fought and the determination and skill with which the traditions of the Royal Regiment of Artillery were maintained by men taking their pieces into action by means and in circumstances very novel to war.

So the fight or rather the siege went on. There was no thought of giving up, even though the chances of relief dwindled with every day that passed.

As late as September 24th, Browning in Nijmegen received a message from Urquhart containing the stout-hearted words "resistance will be continued and we will do our best."

Why relief never came

Why was the Division not relieved ? Why had no unit of the 2nd Army reached the bridge within the planned period of forty-eight hours ? Why, as day after day passed by, did they still linger ? The answer is simple. To reach Arnhem the 2nd Army had to thrust out a long, narrow armoured spearhead, and the units composing it, headed by the Guards Armoured Division, could use but one road, which splits into two soon after leaving the Nijmegen Bridge and joins together again near that of Arnhem. It is a road to advance along which is almost impossible if an enemy wishes to intervene ; for it runs first through orchards of plum and apple with distant poplars decorating the skyline, and then through flat, marshy fields extending to the banks of the Lower Rhine, and it is raised on a causeway some three or four feet above the surrounding country. No tank or armoured vehicle can leave it and not become bogged and, since large stretches are under observation from higher ground, it can be shelled at will as long as that ground remains uncaptured. It was never continuously under Allied control nor free from the enemy's fire. Sometimes it was cut for hours on end ; sometimes the point of the spearhead was blunted by frontal counter attacks. That in a word was why the 1st Airborne Division was not relieved.

Conditions along the road leading through Grave and Nijmegen to the outskirts of Arnhem can be gauged by what happened to Flight Lieutenant Turner, D.F.C., the pilot of a Stirling employed in dropping supplies to the airborne troops. On September 21st he was shot down near Nijmegen and presently arrived there on foot with his crew. Here they were given food, a three-ton lorry, and an order to make for Eindhoven. Five miles from that town they were told that two German tanks - Panthers, it was thought-and a body of S.S. troops were moving against the road from the north-east and would arrive at any moment. "We had two revolvers and a Sten gun between the nine of us," said Turner. Judging this armament insufficient with which to attack tanks, the party drove to Veghel, a small village close by, where they presently fell in with "an Army Lieutenant and three Bofors guns." All at once returned to the main road, determined to fight their way through.

The opportunity to do so soon arrived, for the German tanks made straight for them. The first was knocked out by the Bofors firing at a range of 400 yards, but in the ensuing battle with the second and the S.S. infantry accompanying it, the Army Lieutenant became a casualty, two of the three Bofors were destroyed, and the available ammunition for the third fell to fourteen rounds. So the crew of the Stirling moved off the road once more and joined some thirty British infantry who were without officers but had machine-guns. Though lacking all experience in ground warfare, Turner at once took command. Tiger tanks, suddenly appearing, drove the party back to Veghel, where the lorry, into which they had all clambered, was ambushed and destroyed. Undismayed, the survivors lined a ditch by the roadside, held off the enemy for ten hours with small-arms tire till darkness fell, and then retired with their wounded to a neighbouring house, whose owner gave them all the food he had-one slice of bread and butter and one apple to each man. By then there was almost no ammunition left, and they therefore lay quiet listening to the Germans fifty yards away, who, badly mauled, made no further attack. Late in the next afternoon the advanced guards of the leading British armoured division arrived, and Flight Lieutenant Turner was able to hand over his command, abandon fighting on land, and return eventually to the air, a more familiar element.

Capture of the great bridge at Nijmegen

Such an incident as this shows how fluid and uncertain was the battle raging in the stretch of country separating the British 1st Airborne Division in Arnhem from their American allies and comrades farther south, who were eventually able to make and retain contact with the main body of the 2nd Army. For the Americans had succeeded in all their allotted tasks. By September 19th the 101st Division had seized and was securely holding the bridge at Grave over the Maas, while the 82nd was fighting with magnificent gallantry to capture and hold the great bridge at Nijmegen over the Waal.

On that day, supported by the Guards Armoured Division, it fought one of the fiercest actions of the whole war, having by then been reinforced by the second lift carried in some 400 gliders, which landed within a few hundred yards of the front line.

For twenty-four hours the battle raged with great fury, but the Americans accomplished the seemingly impossible by crossing the Waal in assault boats under withering fire, and eventually seized the northern end of the bridge.

At the same time the Guards attacked the southern end, and soon success crowned the Allied arms. The great tanks roared across the bridge and their crews joined hands with the gallant American parachutists who had judged no price too high for victory. But that was the limit of accomplishment.

Farther north the 2nd Army could not push. Throughout, Lieutenant-General Browning had been in charge of the battle, directing it, first from woods and copses and then from a white house on the outskirts of Nijmegen, where he had arrived with his staff by glider on D day.

It will be remembered that the intention had been to drop most of the Polish Parachute Brigade on a zone immediately south of the bridge at Arnhem. As soon as it was realized that only its northern end was in our hands the zone was moved farther to the west and the Poles eventually landed on the 21st near Driel. Great efforts were then made to take them across the river to reinforce their hard-pressed British comrades. Lieutenant D. Storrs of the Royal Engineers, for example, with tired detachments taken out of the line from all Sapper units in turn, tried for four nights running to ferry them across. On the first night he was quite unable to do so and not a man landed on the other side. On the second night he brought over sixty Poles in rubber dinghies, crossing the river twenty-three times before dawn.

Altogether some 250 Poles passed the river and formed a valuable re-inforcement to the north-eastern corner of the defence. Here they fought with their proverbial gallantry.

Two hundred and fifty men of the Dorsetshire Regiment, part of the 43rd (Wessex) Division, also made most determined efforts to reach Urquhart's men. On the evening of September 22nd, after fighting most of the day, they reached the bank of the river, covering the last ten perilous miles at high speed in lorries, for they knew that behind them the Tiger tanks of the enemy, who had once more broken through, were in cumbersome but determined pursuit. Major H. Parker set booby traps for the Tigers and covered the approaches to the banks with Piats, while the rest of the Dorsets strove to cross the river in "Ducks " (amphibious vehicles) laden with stores and ammunition.

The ground at this point, however, was most unsuitable. The Ducks slithered off the road into the dyke and not one was successfully launched.

On the next day assault boats were used, the battalion carrying them 600 yards through an orchard under heavy mortar and machine-gun fire. Many were hit before they were launched, but a number took the water and into them climbed the men of Dorset. Some, caught in a swift current in midstream, were swept downwards towards the sea ; others were hit and sunk, but by daylight the elements of four companies were on the other side. There, however, they could do little, for they were at once pinned down by heavy tire. They sought to move to higher ground immediately above the river bank and not far from

Oosterbeek, but to reach it they had to climb a slope of sixty degrees. The platoon in the van was led by the commanding officer of the battalion, Lieutenant-Colonel G. Tilly. He was last heard shouting " There they are ! Get at them with the bayonet ! " Then he disappeared, and no trace has been found of him.

All that day the Dorsets fought on in scattered groups, and at one time Major J. D. Grafton called on the guns of the 2nd Army to put down a concentration on his own position which was then filled with the enemy. The shooting was very effective, but neither the Poles nor the Dorsets were able to reach the Airborne Division in numbers large enough to alter the course of the battle. It continued to hold out in its perimeter in conditions which daily, hourly, grew worse.

Fifteen mortar bombs a minute

They were, in fact, almost intolerable to all but troops determined to hold out to the last. Enemy fire varied in intensity, but never by day or night did it cease, though there was apt to be a lull at Sundown. "The Germans always drew stumps at seven o'clock," says Major Wilson. But he adds, "They mortared us continuously at all other times." It was this mortar fire which was especially galling and which accounted for a high proportion of the casualties suffered. Never could anyone feel reasonably safe even in a well-dug and well-sited slit trench. More than one "looked very like a grave," and more than one became a grave. On one small sector alone five mortar bombs fell every twenty seconds, and this rate of fire was often kept up by the enemy for hours at a time.

It would be wrong to maintain that this bombardment had no effect on the spirits of Urquhart's men. It had. As day succeeded day and no relief appeared, and ammunition ran lower and lower till there was almost none at all, to remain cheerful needed a constant effort of the will. The remedy- one which never failed- was to take some action against the enemy.

Sniping became a favourite pastime; and since the standard of marksmanship was high, very few bullets were wasted. "We built a figure out of a pillow with a helmet stuck on one end of it," says Sergeant Quinn of the Reconnaissance Squadron, "and put it on the top of a broom handle. We popped this out now and again, always from a different window, so as to attract German snipers. One of us was watching them from a nearby house -not the house where we were using the dummy. Whenever a sniper showed up, he fired and got him. One of our chaps got fifteen like this, and I got two or three. We were using Stens and Brens. For this work it is best to fire single shots."

Wilson's Independent Parachute Company cut notches on the butts of their rifles for every German killed. One of them returned to England with eighteen. Others stalked tanks and self-propelled guns with Piats. Others, again, who had orders to issue and plans to make, stuck to their task, not allowing the heavy fire to interfere with its fulfilment, and even finding time to note the symptoms which that fire produced. "I found that under such long periods of mortar fire," says Lieutenant-Colonel Mackenzie, G.S.O.1 to the Division, who was to win a D.S.O., "my mind showed a tendency towards lethargy. It was hard to concentrate, and to write anything took a long time." On occasion there would be a lull and the tired men were able to relax for a few precious moments. "In the evening I would go to my trench," said one of them, and smoke a pipe. I used to look at an apple tree which grew nearby and had red apples on it and then I watched the stars come up." Near that spot some 350 years before, another poet, the gentle Philip Sidney, had watched those same stars as he lay dying of a mortal wound.

The R.A.M.C. stays at its post

The wounded were looked after with great devotion by surgeons who remained at their posts to the last and entered captivity or death with them.

The 16th Parachute Field Ambulance, under Lieutenant-Colonel E. Townsend, M.C., was established in the St. Elizabeth Hospital on the evening of the first day, but the Germans reoccupied the buildings a few hours later and took prisoner all the unit save two surgeons, Major Longland and Captain Lipmann-Kessell, who used the greatest ingenuity in preventing their enforced departure. On several occasions when German soldiers arrived with orders to move them, they at once began fresh surgical operations which even the S.S. men were loath to disturb. The two officers remained in the hospital for some weeks until all the wounded there were fit to be taken with them into captivity. The chief medical dressing station was a house not within the perimeter at all but just outside it. Here many of those wounded in the early days of the action were tended. Fighting went on all round this hospital and more than once threatened to invade it. At one p.m. on September 23rd, for example, a German officer under a large Red Cross flag, approached Brigadier Hackett and "threatened that unless our troops withdrew from the house, he would be forced to blow the M.D.S. to pieces. Half an hour later, however, he agreed not to do so provided we did not fire from the immediate vicinity of the hospital." On the next day these threats were renewed, although the Germans were well aware that their own wounded to the number of 150 or more were being cared for by the same doctors.

Eventually many of the wounded, both German and English, were taken by the enemy back into Arnhem. A Regimental Aid Post was established by Captain Martin in Oosterbeek. Conditions in it were very bad, for it was soon housing upwards of 200 wounded, and little beyond first aid could be given to them. The owner of the house, a Dutch lady, worked without rest or food, helped by a boy of seventeen who did likewise. What water there was had to be brought from a pump close by, till it ran "red with blood."

Every evening the lady moved from room to room, her bible in her hand, and in the light of a torch read aloud the 91st Psalm, "for," said she, "it has comforted my children and may comfort you." Lying on mattresses or straw amid the stench of wounds and death, the men heard "her soft voice speaking most carefully the words of King David, 'Thou shalt not be afraid for the terror by night, nor for the arrow that flieth by day, nor for the pestilence that walketh in darkness, nor for the destruction that wasteth at noonday '."

Fire, thirst and hunger were among the tribulations grimly endured. As time wore on, more and more of the houses, so stoutly defended, were set ablaze and became untenable. Hit by a phosphorus bomb, a house usually began to burn in earnest some five minutes later, and this short interval gave to those holding it just time to move to another. After the first forty-eight hours, food became very short, and towards the end was entirely lacking. The Germans cut off the town water supply, and to the pangs of hunger those of thirst were added. "We went four days without food," says Sergeant Quinn, "but we could still get water from a well." In this he and those with him were luckier than most. There were vegetables in the gardens- potatoes, cabbages and some tomatoes -but without water it was difficult to cook them. There were apples to be had from the trees, and some men of the 156th Parachute Battalion "found a bakery and had bread and bottled cherries." The 21st Independent Parachute Company were more fortunate than many of their fellows. "We lived," its commander reports, "on two meals a day, mostly of tinned vegetables. Once a kid ran across the lawn of my headquarters and we killed and ate it."

The cellars of certain houses were found to contain small stocks of food and occasionally of wine, "Champagne, Graves, a light claret and Bols gin." One company filled a bath half full of water before the tap failed and used this for cooking, even after a piece of the ceiling had fallen into it and made it look like "thin; unpleasant porridge." "There just weren't any army rations after the first day," reports an officer, "but there were some tame rabbits, one of which I fed. He used to scratch at the wire of his hutch as I went by, and I'd give him a leaf of lettuce or cabbage. One day a parachutist on the scrounge walked off with my rabbit, dead .... I made him hand it over and left it between my batman's trench and mine, where it got blown to pieces by a shell. Chickens didn't seem to mind the mortaring at all. They lost a few feathers but went on pecking and scratching about quite calmly." Such food as fell from the air went to the Regimental Aid Posts.

"They flew straight into a flaming hell"

Why food and ammunition were not dropped in quantities large enough to keep so comparatively small a body of men supplied is a question which may pertinently be asked. The answer forms a short, tragic, glorious chapter in the history of the Royal Air Force. A zone north west of Arnhem, in the area of Warnsborn, had been chosen as the place on which supplies were to be dropped. Had it been possible to form the perimeter outside the town in accordance with the original plan, this zone would have been well within the lines of the defence. But it was not. As has already been explained the high ground near the zone was never captured, and both remained in the hands of the enemy. A message explaining this was sent by wireless, and a new zone nearer to Oosterbeek indicated. The message with this vital alteration was not received in time. Indeed the great lack of communication between the 1st Airborne Division and Lieutenant General Browning, fighting a hard and successful battle to the south on the Maas and Waal, was more than an inconvenience and sometimes as much as a disaster. This was especially so where the Royal Air Force was concerned. The fact that this extremely important message did not get through, though it was several times repeated, meant that the supply aircraft, Stirlings for the most part together with unarmoured Dakotas, dropped their precious burdens, not upon the airborne troops, but upon their enemies. More than that, to do so they had to encounter very heavy anti-aircraft fire of which the accuracy, since they had to fly low, was high. Unfalteringly they met it.

"Arnhem, 19th September, 1630 hours, " runs the war diary of the Division. "Re-supply dropped on pre-arranged S.D.P. ' V. ' (Supply Dropping Point) which was in enemy's hands. Yellow smoke, yellow triangles and every conceivable means were used to attract attention of pilots and get them to drop supplies within our lines ; this had very limited success." It had indeed. The weather was misty, but the arranged dropping point could be seen and the pilots had eyes for nothing else. "My most poignant memory, " writes Lieutenant-Colonel M. St. J. Packe, in charge of the Royal Army Service Corps elements in Oosterbeek, "will always be the time I spent watching the supply aircraft coming over and dropping their containers on an area not under our control .... They were met by a screen of flak, and it was awe-inspiring to see them fly straight into it, straight into a flaming hell. We thought that some would not face it and would jettison their cargoes, in which case we should get them, for they would fall short and therefore in our lines ; but they all stuck to their course and went on, nor did they hesitate. " A Stirling and a Dakota were seen that day, both on fire, circling round the zone. They were doomed and their pilots knew it, but they might still drop their supplies on the right spot. To do so immediately, however, might interfere with those more fortunate than themselves who were timed to arrive a moment or two before them. So they held off, awaiting their turn. It came, and they went in, blazing, to release the containers ; before they fell "like two torches from the sky," they had done all in their power to ensure success. Such cold-blooded courage is the extreme of heroism. It was prompted, not merely by a strong sense of duty, but also by a feeling of comradeship with those fighting a doughty and perilous battle in the Woods beneath which "looked so quiet and clean," but were full of strife and carnage.

The last hours of resistance

One of the crew of a Stirling, badly hit but still able to fly, looked back at the dropping zone he had just left. "I could see black puffs round the aircraft behind us," he notes in his diary. "It must have been a terrible spot to be in, and we were glad to get out of it. I wondered what sort of battle the airborne men were having and knew it must be tough ; but they had guts and plenty of them. We all wanted to do everything we could to help them." This indeed the Royal Air Force did, as the losses in aircraft testify. On September 18th, the first day on which supplies were dropped, they were six per cent., on the 19th eight per cent., and on the 21st twenty per cent. The average loss during the six days on which flying was possible- on two it was not- was somewhat more than seven per cent. This, though not crippling, was severe. Among the casualties was the leader of the supply aircraft, Wing Commander Davis, D.S.O., who had inspired his crews with a spirit of resolution equal to his own. It is grievous to record that only 7.4 per cent. of the total number of tons dropped was collected by the beleaguered division. For, after the evening of the fifth day, that was what the airborne troops were. "No knowledge of elements of Division in Arnhem for twenty-four hours. Balance of Division in very tight perimeter. Heavy mortaring and machine-gun fire .... Our casualties heavy. Rations stretched to utmost. Relief within twenty-four hours vital. " This is the entry made at 9.44 p.m. on Thursday, September 21st, in the Divisional diary. Yet they held on for another four days. As these went by, it became more and more difficult to move about inside the perimeter. Snipers were active, persistent and ubiquitous, and all the roads were blocked by trunks and branches of trees, bricks and masonry strewn over their surface.

At all times communication between Major-General Urquhart and his Chief, Lieutenant-General Browning, was difficult and often impossible. A large number of the wireless sets carried into action were damaged either on landing or subsequently by enemy action ; a large number were unserviceable almost from the beginning. Throughout the time he spent at the Headquarters of the 1st Parachute Brigade on the outskirts of Arnhem, Urquhart was out of touch for many hours with the 2nd Battalion at the bridge and his own headquarters at Hartestein, though the distance between was not large and was well within the range of the standard equipment carried.

By noon on September 22nd, Urquhart judged it indispensable to send two officers across the Lower Rhine to acquaint Browning with the situation. For this purpose he chose Lieutenant-Colonels C. B. Mackenzie, his G.S.O.1, and E. C. Myers, C.B.E., D.S.O., who was commanding the Royal Engineers. These officers made the crossing under enemy fire in a rubber boat, in company with two others. The boat was inflated in a building at Oosterbeek and dragged over the fields till the river was reached. "I rowed," says Colonel Mackenzie, "and Myers steered .... We parked the boat in a little bay and crawled away from the bank .... There was a battle going on and we couldn't make out which were Poles and which were Germans."

Having found Polish Headquarters, they made what arrangements they could for the Polish Parachute Brigade to be ferried over, but no one was very hopeful, for there was a great lack of boats or materials from which rafts could be built. That evening Mackenzie set off to find the G.O.C.

He went in a reconnaissance car and presently drew near to a windmill, round the corner of which poked "a dirty-looking green nose." It belonged to a Tiger tank, which went at once into action and at the end of the encounter Mackenzie found himself with the reconnaissance car upside down in a ditch.

He crawled away and after some time two Sherman tanks arrived and cleared a passage, so that he was able eventually to speak with General Browning between ten and eleven the next morning. The return journey was made without incident, and he reported to General Urquhart that night, having concerted plans for an evacuation now seen to be inevitable.

CHAPTER 15

"THESE THINGS BEFELL AT ARNHEM"

I t took place on the night of September 25th/26th, and began at ten p.m. The wounded at Divisional Headquarters were left under the care of Lieutenant Randall, R.A.M.C. All doctors and chaplains still alive remained at the Dressing Stations and Regimental Aid Posts. The orders issued were to make as little noise as possible and to reach the river bank in the general area of Oosterbeek, where sappers with assault boats would ferry them across, a distance of between 100 and 150 yards. Many of the men bound pieces of cloth, obtained from houses or from their own uniforms, about their boots, and as soon as it was dark what remained of the Division moved off. The Germans were tired but suspicious. A heavy bombardment, carried out by the guns of the 2nd Army to cover the withdrawal, seems to have been regarded by them as designed to cover the passage of the river in strength by reinforcements. A number of German machine-guns in the woods or on the edge of the fields near Oosterbeek caused a certain amount of confusion. "We heard a German challenge," says one account, "and then a second or two later a blaze of light some fifty yards away, into which, after moving to a flank, we Hung hand grenades."

Soon a queue was forming on the river bank, waiting, in a night jet-black and streaming with rain, for the infantry assault boats, each of which could hold fourteen or fifteen men. A battery of A.A. guns sent red tracer shells across the river to mark the place at which the passage was to be made. They belonged to the Wessex Division and fired a round every minute, alternately in pairs, for seven hours. It was, of necessity, impossible to move them, and each tracer shell that stabbed the darkness betrayed their position. There were too many troops for the boats, some of which were very rickety. Moreover, though comparatively calm near both of its banks, the Lower Rhine was running strongly in the middle.

"We got into a boat," says Lieutenant-Colonel St. J. Packe, "pushed off, and soon reached that part of the river where the current was flowing strongly. I thought that, once in its grip, we would be swept along into what seemed to me to be a hellish battle in progress downstream. At that moment the outboard engine cut, so we seized our rifles and paddled with the butts. I beat time. Those without rifles encouraged those with them until they were persuaded to swop." Many, unable to find a place in the boats, or eager to yield it to a comrade in more evil case than their own, preferred to swim the river. Among them was Siely, the Regimental Sergeant-Major of the Light Regiment. He stayed behind to help late-comers, and it was broad daylight before he began the passage. "I stripped completely," he said, "because I had just seen three men drown, weighed down by their clothes." He got safely across and then made for an old house not far from the south bank, where he assisted his Commanding Officer, who was in the same condition as himself, to assume a lady's blouse. He himself chose "a lady's very nice dark cloth coat."

By noon on September 27th the long ordeal was over. The Division, which had started 10,095 strong, including the glider pilots, had by then lost 7,605 officers and men in killed, wounded and missing. Now at last it was at Nijmegen ; and there, in a large red-brick school in a quiet tree-bordered thoroughfare, an issue of tea, rum, food, and one blanket a man was made. Some who had arrived earlier in the day received a less formal welcome from the sea-borne elements of the Division, who were awaiting them, having advanced some 700 miles through France, Belgium and Holland. Captain Scott

Malden, for example, one of the Divisional Intelligence officers, reached Headquarters clad in several yards of flannel secured by a belt. He was given a breakfast which consisted of half a tumbler of Cointreau, a large bowl of Irish stew, and then a small glass of the same liqueur. After this he slept without moving for twelve hours. Others were provided with the like good cheer, and soon that school at Nijmegen, set aside for their reception, was echoing with the voices of weary men who had passed through an ordeal few have been called upon to face in this war or in any other. They had suffered much, they were weary beyond measure, but they were sustained by that most potent aid to recovery, the knowledge that they had done all and more than their duty.

They walked back to freedom

Behind them, on the other side of the turbid stream, many of their comrades still remained. These belonged to those elements of the Division who had penetrated deeply into Arnhem in an effort to reinforce the 2nd Parachute Battalion at the head of the bridge. Many of them were lying wounded or dead in Arnhem and its outskirts ; many were prisoners, captured in the wrecks of burning houses, their ammunition spent ; but many were wandering among the woods or farms, or hiding in the back streets of the little town. They lived there for weeks, cared for by the Dutch, who to do so showed a spirit of cunning, fortitude and courage which may justly be called sublime.

A great number succeeded in making then way back days and weeks later to the British line. Among them was Brigadier Lathbury, the Commander of the 1st Parachute Brigade. He, it will be remembered, had on his own urgent representations been left wounded and half paralysed in a small house on the outskirts of Arnhem. Its inhabitants took him to the local hospital outside the defensive perimeter. There he was cared for by British surgeons and Dutch nurses, though the enemy was in control. In a day or two he had recovered sufficiently to be able to hobble, and as soon as he realized that the plan had failed and that the 2nd Army would not arrive to capture the town, he crept away at midnight into the woods, walking on a compass bearing in what he hoped was the direction of freedom.

Presently he fell in with a private soldier, and for the best part of a week they remained in the woods, sleeping in a shed and constantly on the move. Another week went by, and he was then put into contact with Mayor A D Tatham-Warter of the 2nd Parachute Battalion, who had been captured by the Germans, escaped from a dressing station, and deliberately returned in order to organise the escape of as many of the Division as could be found still at large. Tatham-Warter showed great aplomb, moving about the district quite freely and so bearing himself that it seemed that the Germans did not suspect him. Once he arrived at the door of a house at the same time as two German soldiers. He glanced sharply at them. They stood aside and allowed him to go in first.

Tatham-Warter and Lathbury fell in with Lieutenant-Colonel Dobie, commanding the 1st Parachute Battalion, and the three men made various plans. Because of the importance of the information he possessed, Dobie was sent ahead and eventually succeeded in making his way with the utmost difficulty to the 2nd Army and safety. The others waited several days and collected stragglers from all over the place. Matters were complicated by the fact that the Germans had decided to evacuate the entire civil population.

The day of the evacuation was that chosen by Lathbury and Tatham-Warter as that on which the parachutists should make their escape. "Our plan worked perfectly .... Eighty officers and men who had been hiding in the area were all assembled at the rendezvous .... To reach it, Tatham-Warter and I cycled along the road side by side, and every time we saw a German- and we passed at least 200, some in groups, some in platoons marching along- I expected to be challenged, but nothing untoward happened."

Forty more other ranks commanded by Major Hibbert, Brigade Major of the 1st Parachute Brigade, were too far away to reach the rendezvous in time, so they were taken there in two lorries. "During the journey they wore their uniforms, carried their weapons and lay flat on the floor of the lorries. They drove straight to the rendezvous, and as they de-bussed, German troops were walking past them on the road." Eventually the whole party reached the bank of the Lower Rhine, and after an anxious forty-five minutes, during which they had a brush with the Germans who evidently mistook them "for a strong patrol," got back across the river aided by the fire of tracer shells.

Twelve days in a cupboard

The adventures of Major A. G. Deane-Drummond, M.C., were even more remarkable. He belongs to the Royal Corps of Signals, and first saw active service as a parachutist in the attack on the aqueduct in Southern Italy in 1941. Taken prisoner then, he twice escaped and eventually came back to his old Division. When they flew to the capture of Arnhem he jumped with the 1st Parachute Battalion, and after a time was sent on to discover, if he could, what was wrong with the wireless sets, for no messages were being received by Divisional Headquarters. He succeeded in putting right those in use at Brigade, then joined a party of forty men in the attack, already described, on the Pavilion near the river.

Long and continuous fighting reduced the numbers of this small force trying to break through to the bridge, and Deane-Drummond eventually found himself alone with his batman in a deserted house. As they were exploring it, a large party of Germans arrived, most of them belonging to an S.S. unit. They put snipers in the upper rooms, and to make sure that they would not desert their posts, locked the doors. In the meanwhile Deane-

Drummond and his batman had gone to ground in the water closet, where they spent the next forty-eight hours. Its door they fastened, and the handle was frequently tried from the outside. No attempt, however, was made to force a way in. Occasionally the Germans lapse into good manners.

When the fighting died away, the two parachute soldiers crept out of their hiding place, muffled their boots with their battle blouses, and crept down the stairs and out of the house, where they separated, intending to meet on the other side of the Lower Rhine. They never did so. Deane-Drummond stripped, tied his clothes in his waterproof jumping smock, and swam the river. After dressing, he began to make his way towards the railway bridge, through an orchard and across some fields. There were Germans all about him, for he could hear them coughing and talking. He went through several lines of slit trenches and had almost reached the railway embankment near the bridge when he fell headlong into a trench on to a German soldier.

Deane-Drummond blew the man's brains out, but "as I lay on top of him another German sprang on me. It seemed certain that I was to be shot, but I suppose the second man did not know his comrade was dead and did not fire for fear of hurting him. Instead of being killed I was made a prisoner."

He did not remain one for very long. Taken back to Arnhem, he watched his opportunity and made off while other parachutists were being rounded up. The refuge he chose was the nearest house, which proved to his misfortune to be some kind of German headquarters. He had just time to bolt into a large, strongly made Dutch cupboard before some S.S. officers entered the room and began to interrogate a number of prisoners. Deane-Drummond spent twelve days in that cupboard, with nothing to eat but a piece of bread and nothing to drink but the contents of his water bottle. At long last another chance came and he slipped away and hid in the garden, being by this time, as he reports, "not a little exhausted." He remained a further three weeks on the wrong side of the Lower Rhine until at last he, too, got safely away.

The men of the parachute and air landing brigades who fell into the enemy's hands were most of them wounded. They were removed to Apeldoorn, and after some days departed thence on foot, or in cattle trucks, to captivity in the interior of the Reich. The wounded received neither food nor medical attention after the first forty-eight hours, when the doctors and the Dutch nurses of Arnhem, who had attended them with unselfish devotion, were no longer allowed to continue their ministrations. Those who survived the journey were deemed fit to work and were accordingly put to labour under blows and unprintable insults in lead-mines. Here they languished until the swift advent of the victorious Allies announced an end to their sufferings. For a moment, however, these were increased, for the prisoners found themselves once again on the march, or jolting in lorries, towards any part of Germany not yet captured. For many that dreadful journey was their last. What the enemy had failed to achieve at Arnhem with Spandaus, self-propelled guns, mortars, tanks, and all the armoury of modern war, he partially succeeded in accomplishing with hunger, thirst and cudgels along the dusty or muddy roads of Germany. For periods as long as fifteen days the men were given but one issue of food, and that consisted of ersatz bread, and more than one batch of prisoners received not even this meagre ration, but were compelled to rely on the non-existent charity of the native inhabitants, Nevertheless, when deliverance came, the courage of the survivors was found to be unbroken. Regimental Sergeant-Major J. C. Lord received his rescuers in a neatly pressed uniform with button bright and shining. His demeanour typifies the spirit that prevailed among the men of Arnhem.

In the treatment of their prisoners the Germans maintained, and enhanced, that reputation for infamous cruelty which they have been at pains to acquire in so many wars through so many centuries.

The Strategic value of Arnhem

With tales of heroism and suffering such as these the story of the 1st Airborne Division in Holland must end ; but the story shows also that as a corporate whole this Division triumphantly vindicated the soundness of their training and proved beyond doubt or dispute that an airborne army is not a luxury but a necessity. On this ground alone the expedition was more than justified; on every other it was abundantly so. For consider the general position of the British armies in the west before and after the battle. Up to September 17th the enemy thought to profit from the tenacious resistance offered by his garrisons in Dunkirk, Lorient, St. Nazaire, and other great French ports. It was denying to the Allies certain links in the chain of supply of vital importance if the pressure of their armies was to be maintained. It seemed to the German High Command that they would be able to use the time thus gained to establish upon the Maas, the Waal and the Lower Rhine, three successive lines on which to stand and fight. They were in the full throes of preparing to do so when out of the skies, which Goering had once boasted would ever belong to the Luftwaffe, a blow fell with devastating suddenness. In the space not of days but of hours this scheme of defence collapsed. At one bound the British 2nd Army leapt nearly sixty miles towards the German frontier and became deeply ensconced in what the enemy had fondly hoped would be his front throughout the winter.

Before a week had passed, the Allies had secured all the bridges over two of the three rivers and possessed that most valuable of all assets in war, a firm base for future operations. .

The enemy's reaction to the airborne attack, though immediate and violent, achieved no more than a limited success. As has been told, he could claim the recapture of the most northerly of the bridges and the thrusting back of the 1st Airborne Division with heavy casualties over the Lower Rhine. This is a fact which must be neither minimized nor exaggerated. The loss of many gallant and highly trained men in an operation of great daring and much hazard must be set against the gain to the general conduct of the campaign as a whole. That this gain was very considerable, no one, not even the enemy, who was constrained to praise the conduct of the Division, will deny.

The resolute seizure of the bridge at Arnhem, which was under British control for three days, combined with the maintenance of a defensive position north of the river for nine days, forced the enemy to devote large resources, among them the remains of two S.S. Panzer Divisions, to the task of ejecting the audacious Urquhart and his men. Had the Germans not been under this necessity, their counter-attacks farther south against the American 82nd and 101st Divisions could have been pressed with much greater vigour and might possibly have succeeded, at least for a time. That they failed must be written largely on the credit side of the ledger when calculating the profit and loss incurred by the operation ; or, to vary the metaphor, because a duellist pierces the chest but not the heart of his adversary, he has not failed in his attack, for he has, none the less, inflicted a grievous, perhaps a mortal wound. For the British 6th and the 17th American Airborne Divisions was reserved the honour of inflicting it on the Germans less than six months later, north of Wesel on the other side of the Rhine. Their swift and overwhelming success would scarcely have been possible if the battle of Arnhem had not been fought.

They fought on, they fought on ...

As for the officers and men of the 1st Airborne Division, what they think of that battle is plain. " Thank you for the party," wrote Brigadier Hackett to General Urquhart afterwards. " It didn't go quite as we hoped and got a bit rougher than we expected. But speaking for myself, I'd take it on again any time and so, I'm sure, would everybody else." That he is right in his surmise no one who reads the story of the 1st Airborne Division at Arnhem can have any doubt. In the tranquil sunshine of an autumn afternoon, its officers and men descended upon territory held in force by the enemy. Some were in action while still falling or gliding through the air, and all were heavily engaged within an hour of landing. From that moment onwards not a man save the dead or desperately wounded but was continuously fighting both by day and by night. They fought in thick woods tearing aside the undergrowth to come to grips with the enemy ; they fought in well ordered streets, in neat houses, in town halls, in taverns, in churches- anywhere where a German was to be found.

With no weapon larger than a seventy five mm gun and for the most part only with Brens, gammon bombs and Piats, which can be carried and handled by one man unaided, they attacked Tiger tanks weighing fifty six tons and self propelled guns with a range of seven miles. Of these they destroyed or put out of action some sixty. The number of the enemy they killed or wounded is not exactly known, but it is not less than 7 000. With no reinforcements save the wounded, who, if their legs would still bear them, staggered back to the firing line, they fought on. With an enemy growing ever stronger, pressing against them on all sides but one- and that a wide, swiftly flowing river they fought on. Without sleep, presently without food or water, at the end almost without ammunition, they fought on. When no hope of victory remained, when all prospect of survival had vanished, when death alone could give them ease, they fought on. In attack most daring, in defence most cunning, in endurance most steadfast, they performed a feat of arms which will be remembered and recounted as long as the virtues of courage and resolution have power to move the hearts of men.

Now these things befell at Arnhem.

CHAPTER 16

THE HIGH ROAD INTO GERMANY

DAWN ON MARCH 24th, 1945, broke clear and bright. The spring sun shone upon air bases in south-east and southern England, lighting the wings of a huge fleet of transport aircraft, tugs and gliders. Two airborne divisions, the British 6th and the American 17th, were before noon to swoop or float down from the sky on to the sullen earth and dark forests of Germany.

One by one in the nimble morning air, the troop carriers, tugs and gliders left the runways, until 1795 of the first and 1,305 of the second appeared over the bridgehead across the Rhine, established in the early hours that morning by 21st Army Group. Of this great fleet, 416 were British aircraft, belonging to 38 and 46 Groups of the Royal Air Force. The first, under the command of Air Vice-Marshal J. R. Scarlett-Streatfeild, C.B.E., took the Air Landing Brigade of the 6th Airborne Division into action ; the second, under Air Commodore L. Darvall, M.C., carried the parachute battalions. The operation upon which these groups were engaged marks the apotheosis of all airborne achievements. Now, at long last, the years of hard endeavour were to be crowned, not merely with success, but with victory, sharp and final as a sword. Now, at last, the successors of Rock and Norman, Lander and Holdson, and of those other gallant pioneers whose tombstones mark the early miles along the road to achievement, were to reach the goal, and, with the indomitable forces of Field-Marshal Montgomery, to deal the enemy a blow from which no recovery was possible. Now, at last, the lessons had been learned and the technique perfected. Before the sun set

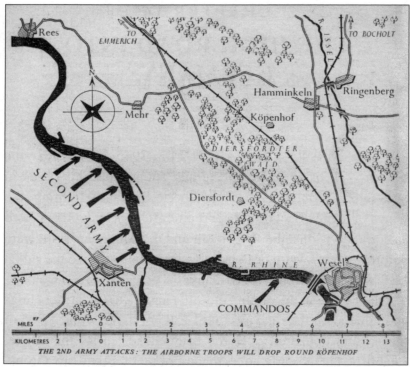

Rees
TO EMMERICH
TO BOCHOLT
R. ISSEL
Hamminkeln
Ringenberg
Mehr
Köpenhof
DIERSFORDTER WALD
Diersfordt
SECOND ARMY
R. RHINE
Wesel
Xanten
COMMANDOS
MILES
KILOMETRES
THE 2ND ARMY ATTACKS: THE AIRBORNE TROOPS WILL DROP ROUND KÖPENHOF

The 2nd Army attacks: the airborne troops will frop around Köpenhof

upon that day, the gates were down and the way to the heart of the Reich lay open.

To describe the operation in detail was not possible at the moment of writing, for the men who carried it out were still in action, a hundred and fifty miles or more beyond the spot where their feet first touched German soil. How they were able to do so with but a fraction of the losses sustained in the light at Arnhem ; how, in a few short days, they took their place in the forefront of a victorious army, sweeping over Germany with a speed which Murat's horsemen in 1806 would have envied and applauded, deserves a short examination.

The achievement was no mere stroke of luck, no happy combination of bravery and good fortune. It was the result of experience gained in operations which had taken the men who wear the red beret to the stony hills of Africa, the dusty olive-yards of Sicily, the green pastures of Normandy, the trim fields and ordered woods of Holland. At each of these battlefields something new had been learned, some theory proved or found wanting.

The result was distilled into the essence of victory and poured over the Rhine.

It had always been held that the sudden, swift descent behind hostile lines of several thousand airborne troops, whose deficiency in heavy arms is, in the early stages at least, more than compensated by the high degree of their training, would set an enemy a problem in defence to which he might not be able to find the answer in time to avoid defeat. A fourth front or flank is thereby created, literally " out of the blue," and it is formed in that most vulnerable quarter of an army, its rear. Such an attack may have serious, perhaps fatal, consequences. Thus, in the Netherlands in 1940, it was German parachutists who made all effective resistance impossible in the space of a few days ; and four years later it was British and American parachutists who gave puissant, indeed invaluable, aid to the seaborne invaders of the French coast. Yet, when an operation greater than any of these was attempted at Arnhem, Nijmegen and Grave, it was successful only at the second and third of these objectives. Despite all the majestic gallantry of the 1st Airborne Division, the bridge at Arnhem could not be held.

The American airborne troops had been successful at Grave and Nijmegen because it had been possible for them to join with the land troops before the enemy had mustered sufficient strength to drive them off the bridges which they had captured. In other words, the strength and protection which heavy guns and heavy tanks can afford to infantry was available just, and only just, in time. This was not so at Arnhem : there the armour and the guns were unable to move in sufficient strength or fast enough along the single available road and no link was made.

The planners of the operation which was to put airborne

forces on the other side of the Rhine took counsel in the fierce light of this experience.

They decided to give those forces the maximum degree of protection which could be afforded, not after the first twenty-four or forty-eight hours, but from the very outset. The plan, therefore, provided that the 6th Airborne Division, landing on German soil north of Wesel, would always be within range of the medium artillery of 21st Army Group. More than that, when they arrived, there would already be many units of that group across the river and very close to the ground which they were to occupy. Major General Matthew B. Ridgeway, of the United States Army, in Command, with General Gale, commanding the 1st British Airborne Corps, as his Deputy, Air Marshal Sir Arthur Coningham, and the other planners reversed, . in fact, the usual procedure up till then followed. At "H" hour on March 23rd/24th, the land armies would form the van. The parachutists and air landing troops would come last. It was a bold stroke, which, though it might mean a high rate of casualties at touch-down, nevertheless would, it was hoped, achieve complete tactical surprise.

That the enemy was expecting landings from the air was well known. A German order captured some weeks before displayed the scheme which the German High Command had adopted to deal with Allied airborne troops attacking on the plan followed in Sicily, Normandy and Holland. Small combat groups of well-trained, efficient soldiers, belonging mostly to the German Parachute and S.S. formations, were to be stationed at all spots where a landing from the air might reasonably be expected. Their duty was to attack the airborne troops at the moment when they were least able to resist- when, having abandoned their parachutes, they were forming up into their combat units, or when they were hacking their way out of the gliders, dragging with them their indispensable weapons. At such a time, the airborne soldier is relatively helpless. lf, however, he arrives on

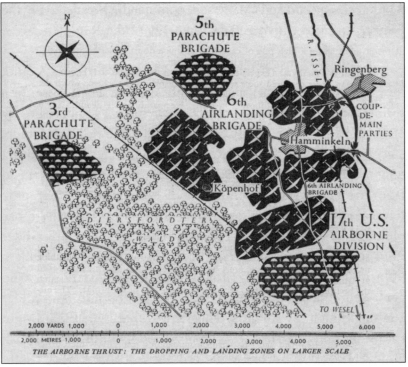

The airborne thrust: the dropping and landing zones on a larger scale.

the heels of an artillery bombardment at a moment when his opposite is either committed or about to join battle with attackers advancing on the ground, the enemy is at once confused, for there are two foes to fight ; one in front, the other immediately behind, or actually upon him.

To give immediately the protection which ground troops can afford to airborne, instead of some hours later, did not, however, suffice. Something more was necessary. There must be no long approach march as happened at Arnhem when, for example, Frost's 2nd Parachute Battalion had to march the best part of eight miles to seize the northern end of the bridge. The airborne troops must land as close as possible to their immediate objectives, and they must land, not concentrated in one special area, which it would be relatively easy to defend, but all over the place and from every direction at once. Was this possible ?

Scarlett-Streatfeild and Chatterton, commanding respectively the Carrier Air Forces involved and the Glider Pilot Regiment, were sure that it was.

Their crews and their pilots, already most efficient, could, they felt certain, be still more highly trained. They were. In a series of exercises carried out from December 1944 to February 1945, they learned not only how to reach the area-an art which, since most of them were veterans, they had already acquired-but how to land on one special spot in that area, chosen beforehand from the multitudinous photographs which the Photographic Reconnaissance Units of the Royal Air Force, especially those of the 2nd Tactical Air Force, had provided. Chatterton's Glider Pilot Regiment had been reinforced after its losses at Arnhem by a high proportion of pilots of the Royal Air Force, who contrived, in a short space of time, to learn both to fly a glider and then taught as soldiers. Thus it was that, when that bright spring morning dawned, every pair of pilots in the 440 British gliders who took off knew not only how to fight, but exactly where to fight.

Two other features were also introduced into the plan and made powerful contributions towards its success. First, General Brereton, commanding the 1st Allied Airborne Army, was determined that his divisions should be taken to their destination in one " lift," and that the airborne supplies destined for their use should be dropped not twelve or twenty-four hours after their landing, when the enemy might have had time to recover somewhat and to organise his defences, but on the very same evening, six hours at most after the landings had been completed. The procedure which had caused such heavy casualties and such gallantry at Arnhem was not to be repeated.

Secondly, since the success of the airborne assault depended on strict nicety of timing, the guns of General Dempsey 's 2nd Army were to make a special effort, in conjunction with the Royal Air Force, to neutralize all known enemy flak positions

and were to continue to fire upon them to within a few minutes
of the hour at which the first landings were to be made.

The first tactical air landing of the war

The plan for the landings itself had been conceived as early
as October 1944, when it became evident that the crossing of the
Rhine in the Wesel area was highly desirable and would, if
successful, have a profound effect on the general course of the
campaign in the West. Major-General Ridgeway was in
command, with General Gale as his Deputy. The 6th Airborne
Division was under the command of Major-General E. Bols,
D.S.O. Their plan was as follows : It had been known for some
time that the Germans had two weak divisions in the sector
chosen for attack, the 7th Parachute Division to the north, the
84th Infantry to the south, and that their only reinforcements
were a number of hastily improvised units, one of them
composed of special anti-airborne troops. The leading Corps of
21st Army Group had been ready for some weeks to cross the
Rhine, and was completely confident of its ability to do so. Its
subsequent progress, however, might be difficult, because, after
crossing the eastern bank of that river, the plain in which it would
fight was dominated by the high ground forming the western
edge of the Diersfordter Wald. This wooded stretch of hills had
to be captured at all costs, and this was the primary task of the
airborne troops.

Beyond it, nearer by some miles to the interior of Germany,
runs the River Issel, traversed on the front of the British 6th
Airborne Division by one railway and two road bridges. To seize
and hold them would mean that the path to the heart of Western
Germany, and beyond, to Berlin itself, would lie open. These
bridges, then, had to he seized, and by capturing them and the
Forest of Diersfordter, the British 6th and the American 17th
Airborne Divisions would very greatly increase and accelerate
the build-up of the attacking forces crossing the Rhine by

buffalo, boat and other means. The specific task of the 6th Airborne Division was apportioned between the Parachute Brigades and the Air Landing Brigade. The 3rd and 5th Parachute Brigades, under their tried Commanders, Brigadiers J. Hill, D.S.O., and R. Poett, D.S.O., were to land on the northern flank of the area to be captured and to hold it against enemy counter-attack ; while the 6th Air Landing Brigade, under Brigadier R. H. Bellamy, D.S.O., was to seize the bridges and contain the village of Hamminkeln. The artillery and other divisional troops were to land in the centre of the area.

To put this plan into operation meant that the 6th Airborne Division would have to carry out the first tactical as opposed to strategic air landing of the war. Both their Parachute Battalions and their air landing troops would have to land either very close to, or actually upon, their objectives. To make it easier for the second to do so, a new type of glider, the Horsa Mark II, was to be used. This aircraft, like the Hamilcar, possesses a hinged nose which, as soon as a landing has been made, can be swung back, thus enabling the material stowed in its belly-a jeep or anti-tank gun-to be driven straight out on to the ground and immediately into action.

The air forces detailed to carry the division belonged to No. 38 and No. 46 Groups, of which the second is part of Transport Command and played a conspicuous part in the three major airborne operations directed against Europe-the landings in Normandy, Holland and Germany. Originally formed in February 1944, under the command of Air Vice-Marshal Fiddament, C.B.E., D.F.C., its pilots and crews acquired in three months an amount of skill and training which it would normally need a year to absorb. It was this group which carried many of the parachute troops who landed in Normandy, and subsequently kept them supplied and evacuated many thousands of wounded between June 1944 and the attack on Arnhem. During the operations round and over the town of Arnhem, its unarmed, vulnerable and slow Dakotas had sought unflinchingly to supply the 1st Airborne Division throughout the course of their desperate battle, and their conduct was such that it called forth from a glider pilot in action on the ground the observation that "we were humbled by the audacity of the re-supply pilots." At last, a spectacular opportunity to be of service was to be afforded this hardworking Group.

The process of rendering the enemy incapable of making a sustained or effective counter-attack had to be initiated and pursued for several weeks ; here the heavy bombers of Bomber Command and of the 8th and 9th American Army Air Forces were able to play a very important part. Between them, they carried out an almost continuous attack ; first on communications, and then on the immediate battle area. Their assistance was impartially bestowed on airborne and land troops alike. Roads, railways, marshalling yards, bridges were remorselessly pounded, two spans of the important Bielefeld Viaduct, for example, being wiped out by one bomb which weighed 22,000 pounds. These attacks reached a culminating point on March 12th, when 1,100 heavy bombers dropped over 5,400 (United States) tons of bombs on Dortmund. As the day of the crossing drew nearer, the tempo increased, and to transport and communication targets were added barracks and military positions. In all these attacks, Coningham's incomparable 2nd Tactical Air Force played a leading, a vital part. Finally, ten airfields of the Luftwaffe received over 2,700 tons of bombs on March 21st and 22nd, while fifty-two enemy aircraft were shot down in combat and 116 destroyed on the ground. So much for the preliminary process of subduing the enemy.

The efforts made immediately before and during the battle to quell his flak positions were equally, if not more, severe. Medium, light and lighter bombers had been paying special attention to such targets for some time beforehand, and on the day of the operation twenty-three of these positions received some 800 tons of bombs. That day over 7,700 sorties were made by the air forces of Britain and the U.S.A., and this figure does not include those flown by the troop carriers and their escort. Here in truth was displayed, in all its grim majesty, the air power of the Allies. So effective was it and so lethal the fire of Montgomery's guns, that such casualties as were caused to tugs, gliders and troop carriers were almost all " due to light flak and small arms fire, the heaviest concentration of which was experienced by the forces that turned left to the north of the landing areas."

So much for the preliminary operations and the plan. The manner of its execution demonstrates, beyond possibility of doubt, what skill combined with high courage can achieve.

"I could see the Rhine"

For many days before the take-off, most elaborate and meticulous preparations had been made for the pilots and crews of the Royal Air Force, under the operational command of Air Vice-Marshal Scarlett-Streatfeild, to take the Division to its destination. Each pilot of each tug, glider and troop carrier had been given an individual briefing, and all knew the exact route and the exact time at which it would be necessary to cast off. For days before the briefing took place it had become apparent to the officers and men of the Group that something portentous was in the wind. Before the end of February, Scarlett-Streatfeild had instructed all his Station Commanders that every aircraft must be available within a very short space of time. All crews, whose tour of duty had, or was about to, come to an end, were required to continue on operations. All " screened " pilots- those, that is, who having completed one or more tours of service are occupied in the task of instructing- were released for active duty. The more advanced of their pupils, twenty crews in all, were hastily but efficiently trained in the task of towing a glider for a maximum of four hours in a daylight operation to a known objective. The Air Vice-Marshal did not hesitate to demand a serviceability of one hundred per cent., and knowing his men, he obtained it. Out of the 320 aircraft in 38 Group ready for the operation, 320 took off and all but one reached the neighbourhood of the objective.

This achievement would not have been possible had not the ground staff shown the same efficient enthusiasm which marked the conduct of their flying comrades. No tow rope failure has been reported, and in one airfield alone, seventy-one newly delivered Halifaxes of the latest type were made ready for the operation by men working without pause until the job was done. The result was apparent at the moment of take-off, when sixty combinations left the ground in fifty-six minutes. It is pleasant to record that fifty-eight of them returned ; one was shot down in flames and one made a forced landing in France, with its control column almost severed and hastily repaired with the shaft of a hammer bound to it by the Flight Engineer.

The great team of tugs and gliders took off in the early hours of March 24th, 1945. Their rendezvous was over Hawkinge in Kent. Thence the aerial fleet set course for Brussels, and passing over the field of Waterloo, turned northwards and was soon crossing the Meuse. "From there," says Brigadier G. K. Bourne, O.B.E., "I could see the Rhine, a silver streak, and beyond it a thick, black haze, for all the world like Manchester or Birmingham as seen from the air. For the moment, I wondered whether the bombing of Wesel, which had preceded the attack upon that town by Commando troops, had been mis-timed. If this was so, then the whole landing zones would be obscured by the clouds of dust which would be blowing from the rubble created by the attack." Dusty they were, but that did not prevent the pilots from making a very successful landing. By 9.45 a.m. the fleet was approaching its objectives ; over the Rhine it flew, at a height of 2,500 feet, and three hours and ten minutes after the first of the combinations had taken off, the first glider was released.

"In accordance with orders, but against my will, for I wanted to see what was happening, I had strapped myself in," Brigadier Bourne goes on. "We began to go down in a steep glide, and I listened with strained interest to the excited converse of our two pilots, neither of whom had been on operations before .... Presently, I heard the first pilot say to the second 'I can see the railway.' Then I felt much relieved, and soon I saw the landscape flying past the windows. We landed very fast, went through a couple of fences and stopped with a jerk. All of us, consisting of the Defence Platoon of Divisional Headquarters, nipped out and took cover under a low bank on top of which was a post and rail fence. There was a lot of shooting about a mile away. We had arrived only about 600 yards from the pre-ordained spot." They moved off, reached two farms outside which German prisoners standing in docile lines were observed, and presently reached their Headquarters at Kipenliof Farm. Throughout, sniping was heavy from the eastern edge of the Forest.

Some gliders landed within 200 and others within 50 yards of the objective; and this, despite an artificial haze, created by the bombardment and the bombing of Wesel which, in places, reduced the length of vision to less than a furlong. Some landings were more, others less, eventful. The gliders carrying the coup-de-main parties of the Royal Ulster Rifles and the Oxfordshire and Buckinghamshire Light Infantry were particularly successful. The first, consisting of a party carried in six gliders, landed with pin-point accuracy on both sides of the bridge over the Issel-their objective; the second only on the west side of the second bridge, but it was speedily captured, though it had subsequently to be blown in order to prevent a German counter attack at night headed by a Tiger tank.

Despite the careful planning and execution of the operation, the unforeseen played its inevitable and important part-this time, mostly in the Allies' favour.. Thus it happened that many of the 513th Parachute Regiment of the American Army dropped by mistake on the divisional landing zone some little time before the gliders arrived. The Americans did not waste a moment checking their exact whereabouts, but went immediately, and with the utmost resolution, into action against a bewildered but still fiercely resisting enemy. Casualties were not light, but by the time the British gliders began to swoop towards the ground, they had done "wonderful work."

In the words of one who saw them that day "they were not just good fighters, they were very good."

Of those landing by glider, the least fortunate were the Oxfordshire and Buckinghamshire Light Infantry, the Light Regiment of Royal Artillery and the Detachments of Royal Engineers. Several of the gliders carrying these went astray, and soon expert Sappers were at a premium. The Commander of the Royal Artillery, Brigadier C. K. T. Faithfull, who had walked out uninjured from a glider reduced to matchwood by the force of its landing, found himself with no staff and but one signals officer to help him. Nevertheless; the guns were successfully fought, and the Sappers completed all their demolition tasks, though at the outset hardly more than a quarter of their numbers were available.

Of the gliders which carried these troops and the Air Landing Brigade, 90 per cent touched down in the landing zone ; but of the 416 which reached the battlefield only 88 landed undamaged. Of the remainder, all were hit, mostly by light flak and small arms fire, and 37 were completely burned out.

The casualties among the glider pilots amounted at the end of that day to between 20 and 30 per cent. killed, wounded and missing.

The winged horse and its rider

While the Air Landing Brigade was thus coming into action and securing its objectives, the rest of the Division, composed of the 3rd and 5th Parachute Brigades, was equally successful.

They reached their landing zones under tire which, although heavy, and indeed severe, came mostly from light flak.

The drop was accurate, and they were at once in action against an enemy who were, for a time, determined to sell their lives dearly. Poett's men of the 5th Parachute Brigade attacked them in that spirit of genial ferocity which is the hallmark of airborne troops. Throughout this action, the high music of hunting horns, which have long been used by the commanders to rally their men, sounded up and down the battlefield, and the German defenders of the position discovered a new and pregnant meaning to the French poet's observation that "le son du cor est triste au fond des bois."

By that evening, the parachute troops had so overcome the enemy that it was possible for some at least of them to relax for a moment from their labours. Lieutenant-Colonel P. Luard, D.S.O., commanding the 13th Battalion of the 5th Parachute Brigade, cooked scrambled eggs for his Divisional Commander in the kitchen, festooned with smoked hams, of the farmhouse which he had made his headquarters; and one of Brigadier Poett's staff -in private life a jockey- provided jugs of milk from the neighbouring cows. The 3rd Parachute Brigade, under Brigadier J. Hill, took somewhat longer to clear the woods which surrounded their allotted objectives, but by early afternoon they had fought round them and captured between six and seven hundred prisoners.

By one o'clock in the afternoon the Division had captured all their objectives, and by midnight Major-General Ridgeway had been able to pay them a visit. At ten a.m. the next morning, March 25th, the link between the airborne forces and the 2nd Army on the ground was strong and unbreakable.

So ended the first phase of the operation, which was conspicuously successful. The reason is not far to seek. The lessons taught by previous bloody, hard-fought battles had been well and truly learned, and the airborne troops had gone into action tied closely in terms of time and space to the army on the ground. The result was victory, unadulterated and complete. It must not, however, be thought that its achievement was easy and almost bloodless.

Despite the days and weeks of preparation, despite the novelty of the plan, despite the careful and accurate bombing and artillery fire, somewhat more than a thousand out of a total of about 8,000 were casualties by sundown.

Here the story of the exploits of the 6th Airborne Division must end, at the moment of their greatest triumph, the seizure of the high ground across the Rhine and of the bridges across the Issel. This achievement opened the flood gates, and in a few days the tide of Montgomery's embattled might flowed through. The triumph was not theirs only, but belonged also to their gallant comrades of the 17th U.S. Airborne Division who fought beside them that day, and also, if indirectly, to the 1st British Airborne, who bore the burden of the day in Africa, Sicily and Holland. The high esteem in which the nation holds those men had received due expression on Wednesday, December 6th, 1944, at a special Investiture held in Buckingham Palace. There, in the main hall, with its wide, crimson carpet, its pillars of white and gold, and its glimpse beyond of a gallery adorned with pictures of famous battles fought and won in other ages, the King bestowed the rewards of valour on some of those who had fought at Arnhem. The deeds they performed in that town were an inspiration and a spur to the men of the 6th Airborne, to whom was granted the good fortune to be the first of the airborne forces to set foot in Germany. Each officer and man of these two divisions wears upon his shoulder the badge of Pegasus, the winged horse and its rider, brandishing a lance. As an emblem it is singularly appropriate, and whenever the citizens of Britain catch sight of it, they may perhaps call to mind that other horse which, long ago, it is said, brought armed men into the city of Troy- the vanguard of a victorious army.

MORE FROM THE SAME SERIES

Most books from the 'World War II from Original Sources' series are edited and endorsed by Emmy Award winning film maker and military historian Bob Carruthers, producer of Discovery Channel's Line of Fire and Weapons of War and BBC's Both Sides of the Line. Long experience and strong editorial control gives the military history enthusiast the ability to buy with confidence.

The series advisor is David McWhinnie, producer of the acclaimed Battlefield series for Discovery Channel. David and Bob have co-produced books and films with a wide variety of the UK's leading historians including Professor John Erickson and Dr David Chandler.

Where possible the books draw on rare primary sources to give the military enthusiast new insights into a fascinating subject.

For more information visit www.pen-and-sword.co.uk